MOROCCAN JEWS
IN FRANCE AND CANADA

MOROCCAN JEWS IN FRANCE AND CANADA

Yolande Cohen

University of Ottawa Press
2025

Les **Presses** de l'Université d'Ottawa
University of Ottawa **Press**

Les Presses de l'Université d'Ottawa / University of Ottawa Press (PUO-UOP) is North America's flagship bilingual university press, affiliated to one of Canada's top research universities. PUO-UOP enriches the intellectual and cultural discourse of our increasingly knowledge-based and globalized world with peer-reviewed, award-winning books.

www.Press.uOttawa.ca

Library and Archives Canada Cataloguing in Publication

Title: Moroccan Jews in France and Canada / Yolande Cohen.
Names: Cohen, Yolande, author
Description: Includes bibliographical references.
Identifiers: Canadiana (print) 20250237792 | Canadiana (ebook) 20250237806
 | ISBN 9780776645148 (softcover) | ISBN 9780776645155 (hardcover) |
 ISBN 9780776645179 (PDF) | ISBN 9780776645162 (EPUB)
Subjects: LCSH: Jews, Moroccan—Canada. | LCSH: Jews, Moroccan—France. | LCSH: Immigrants—Canada. | LCSH: Immigrants—France. | LCSH: Canada—Emigration and immigration. | LCSH: France—Emigration and immigration.
Classification: LCC FC106.J5 C56 2025 | DDC 305.8924071—dc23

Legal Deposit: Fourth Quarter 2025
Library and Archives Canada

© University of Ottawa Press 2025
All rights reserved

No part of this publication may be reproduced or transmitted in any form or by any means, or stored in a database and retrieval system, without prior permission.

Production Team
Copy editing   Céline Parent
Proofreading   Tanina Drvar
Typesetting   Nord Compo
Front cover design Benoit Deneault
Cover layout   Dany Lagueux

Cover Image   Elena Ray, *The Protective Hand of Fatima Also Known as Hamsa*, ID 25593156, Dreamstime.com.

We wish to acknowledge the Social Sciences and Humanities Research Council of Canada, the Faculty of Social Sciences and the Department of History at the University of Quebec in Montreal, as well as the Israel and Golda Koschtizky Centre for Jewish Studies at York University for their generous support of this publication.

---

uOttawa

PUO-UOP gratefully acknowledges the funding support of the University of Ottawa, the Government of Canada, the Canada Council for the Arts, the Ontario Arts Council and the Government of Ontario.

To Marcel,
To Sara and Lorne
To Nathan, Anne-Sarah and Penelope

Table of Contents

List of Figures ix
List of Tables xi
Acknowledgements xiii
Introduction 1

Historiographical Framework

Scholarship on Moroccan Jews in Canada:
Multidisciplinary, Multilingual, and Diasporic 9
Yolande Cohen and Stephanie Tara Schwartz

PART I
The Jews of Morocco and Their Departures

CHAPTER 1
From Synagogue to Mosque: My Grandfather's House
in the Old Mellah of Meknès 27
Yolande Cohen and Noureddine Harrami

CHAPTER 2
Zionism, Colonialism, and Post-Colonial Migrations:
Moroccan Jews' Memories of Displacement 41
Yolande Cohen

PART II
Between Paris and Montreal

CHAPTER 3
Marriage and Mobility of Moroccan Jews
in Montreal and Paris 59
Yolande Cohen and Martin Messika

CHAPTER 4
Sephardi Jews in Montreal 73
Yolande Cohen

PART III
Memoirs of Migration in Canada

CHAPTER 5
Memories of Departures: Stories of Jews
from Muslim Lands in Montreal 89
Yolande Cohen, Martin Messika, and Sara Cohen Fournier

CHAPTER 6
Forgetting and Forging: My Canadian Experience
as a Moroccan Jew 107
Yolande Cohen

CHAPTER 7
A Piece of a Torah Scroll in My Basement 119
Yolande Cohen

Bibliography 123

List of Figures

Figure 7.1. A Piece of a Torah Scroll. 121

List of Tables

Table 3.1. "How connected are you to Jewish life in your city?" (2018, percentage).............................. 61

Table 3.2. Occupational distribution of Moroccan-Jewish men in Montreal (1969–2014, percentage)................ 69

Table 3.3. Occupational distribution of Moroccan-Jewish women in Montreal (1969–2014, percentage)........... 70

Acknowledgements

This volume (along with the companion volume that presents my essays in French) is the result of a large research project, which was funded by generous grants from the Social Sciences and Humanities Research Council (2014–2024). Entitled "Moroccan Jews Migrations to Canada and France from 1948 till Now: An Individual, Communal, Diasporic, and Transnational Incorporation?," this research mobilized a number of people to contribute to this collective work. Without this funding, I would not have been able to gather a team of incredibly talented students and assistants who helped me work through a trove of archives, gather as many oral histories as possible, and write many comparative essays on both France and Quebec/Canada.

I want to sincerely thank my co-authors who readily gave me their agreement to publish the essays we wrote together in this book: Sara Cohen Fournier, the late Noureddine Harrami, Martin Messika, and Stephanie Tara Schwartz. This is the beginning of a new journey for our research to reach another public.

I am indebted to many people, students, colleagues, and friends who have spent their time and effort with me, in order to realize this vast endeavour. I had the privilege of supervising a large team of students and research assistants, including Linda Guerry, Christine Chevalier Caron, and Martin Messika, who helped me develop a project that took several decades of collective work to achieve. Many contributed to this work, at one point or another during their graduate studies at Université du Québec à Montréal (UQAM): Kellie Lacasse, Sabrina Choinière, Guillaume Sellier, Olivier Bérubé Sasseville, Philippe Néméh Nombré, Nicolas Jodoin, and others. Many thanks also to Emilien Tortel, doctoral student at UQAM, who helped me put the manuscript together, reading and rereading the final drafts. The essays gathered in this volume present the result of this work.

Steven High was instrumental in helping me think through my own research in different terms, revealing to me the traumas of my own migration, thereby helping me understand Moroccan Jews' traumas in the post-Shoah period. Working with him, and the team he assembled for the SSHRC funded project *Montréal Life Stories*, was indeed a wonderful experience. We shared many years of intense work, learning how to share our authority as academics and researchers with the many communities that contributed so intensely to our historical writing. At Concordia University, the Centre for Oral History hosts *Montréal Life Stories*, where those interviews are stored and made available to the public. Our previous interviews on Moroccan Jews can be found at the Alex Dworkin Canadian Jewish Archives, where most of my personal archives are also stored.

I also thank my dear colleagues, in my department and at the Faculty of the Humanities and Social Sciences at UQAM for their indefectible support, both moral and financial. My sincere thanks go also to the international team of colleagues and friends, which form an invaluable intellectual network that gave me the incentive to pursue this work. Many thanks to the anonymous readers that reviewed the essays presented here (for all our publications, see our team's publication list in the bibliography section). My friend and esteemed colleague James Jackson was kind enough to help me with the English version of my introduction to this volume.

I also want to thank Pierre Anctil, who was one of the first supporters of my research and is the director of the series in which both the English and French volume are published. My sincere thanks to Mireille Piché for all her hard work on the manuscripts, which I submitted to the University of Ottawa Press, to Maryse Cloutier for supervising the production process, and to Céline Parent for her meticulous and detailed attention to the minutiae in proof-reading and correcting this volume.

I also wish to extend my gratitude and thanks to David Koffman, the J. Richard Shiff chair for the study of Canadian Jewry, and the Israel and Golda Koschtizky Centre for Jewish Studies at York University for their generous support of this publication.

Introduction

When I first started working on the tiny Montreal Moroccan-Jewish community, I did not envision that it would bring me to document such a broad global history. From my first interviews of my neighbours and friends in the 1980s to the essays that appear in this volume, I uncovered many layers of meaning and understanding of this community's hectic trajectory. From their departure from Morocco to their arrival in France and Canada, Moroccan Jews faced many challenges. In the following pages, we highlight their trajectories and paths of migration; their long and difficult journey was less a departure from point A to point B than a series of transnational migrations and circulations.

Why did they leave Morocco? When did this migration happen? And how can we analyze their journey? The period and context of their departure are fraught with complex issues. As colonial subjects of the French Empire, they were treated as "indigenes" in need of "regeneration." Yet if some of them believed in French emancipation, it came to a brutal end with the implementation of the Vichy regime's antisemitic laws in Morocco in 1942. With the ending of the French colonial empire and the decolonization process, Moroccan Jews' rupture with France was (almost) complete. After the establishment of the State of Israel and the subsequent Israel-Arab wars, they joined in the mass exodus of Jews from Arab lands, leaving their countries to join refugee camps in the post-Shoah resettlement of survivors in Europe. In this context, the fate of the large Moroccan-Jewish community became an object of interest for the French, Moroccan, and Israeli states, as well as international Jewish organizations (Cohen and Tortel, 2025). Canada had not yet begun to become an active player, reacting only when the federal government came under mounting pressure from the Canadian Jewish Congress to open its doors to North African Jewish refugees.

This volume presents the many different aspects of Moroccan Jews' migration to France and Canada and incorporation in those two countries following the Second World War, starting with a historiographical overview. This largely francophone population, based in Montreal, has received relatively little attention from Canadian scholars. The study of Montreal's Moroccan Jews is found primarily in articles and books dealing with Quebec studies, and the Jewish diaspora, all generally published in French. Further, it offers an exemplary case study of the difficulties minority groups in Canada, and specifically in Quebec, face in vying for a place in the national narrative, despite years of public discourse about their inclusion.

As Stephanie Tara Schwartz and I demonstrate, the study of Moroccan Jews in Canada, part of a broader field of Sephardic, Mizrahi, and Arab-Jewish studies, is mainly transnational. First assimilated within the Jewish landscape while trying to establish their distinct Sephardic identity, Moroccan Jews were torn between divergent forces of Quebec nationalism and Canadian multiculturalism, before finding a feeble but steady voice through religion and transnational dialogue with the wider Sephardic-Mizrahi diaspora. Often reduced to folklore and nostalgic memory, Moroccan Jews insist on their cultural and religious traditions; there is still a long way to go before historians incorporate this population's particular experience within the global history of Canada.

There is also a need to include their story in the overall history of transnational migrations. Among the masses of migrant populations driven to leave their countries against the backdrop of European decolonization, North African Jews occupy a special place.[1] Several studies have examined the conditions under which these populations migrated (Stillman, 1979; Abitbol, 1989; Laskier, 1994; Kenbib, 1994; Trigano, 2009). Nonetheless, historians do not agree on the reasons that motivated Jews to leave North Africa (and Morocco in particular), which led to the near-total disappearance of two-millennia-old Jewish communities

---

[1] In 1948, the Jewish population of North Africa comprised around 550,000 people. In the 1980s, this figure had dropped to only 30,000 people. Nearly 20,000 North African Jews emigrated to Canada; 230,000 settled in France (120,000 of Algerian origin, 65,000 from Tunisia, and 55,000 from Morocco); and 300,000 in Israel. Jacques Taïeb, "Immigrés d'Afrique du Nord : Combien ? Quand ? Pourquoi ?," in *Terre d'exil, terre d'asile. Migrations juives en France aux XIXe et XXe siècles*, ed. Colette Zytniki (Paris: Éditions de l'Éclat, 2010), 149–154.

from Islamic countries. Martin Messika, Sara Cohen Fournier, and I show that Moroccan Jews' migrations have raised multiple interpretations concerning their departure/dispersion/exile. The multiple strands of Moroccan Jews' history have yet to be gathered into a single main narrative. In this essay, we show what memories and perceptions are conveyed by the migrants we have interviewed over the last three decades in France and in Canada.

Eager to better understand Moroccan Jews' multiple trajectories, and in search of a more nuanced interpretation, I explored my own family migration history. How can we explain the uprooting of an entire community in such a short period of time? What are the effects of this massive displacement?

Attending a conference in my hometown of Meknès, I went back to my grandfather's home in the Jewish old quarters, with my late colleague and friend Noureddine Harrami. Together, we walked through the streets where once stood the shops my grandfather owned, the synagogue he attended, and the homes of his friends. He never left Meknès, where he now lies buried with his beloved wife in his hometown's beautiful cemetery. The family that bought his house remembers him and greets with warmth many members of my own family, who go there on pilgrimage. In our encounter, they talk about their own perceptions of my grandfather and of the times when Muslims and Jews shared common ways of life and work, whereas now Jews have completely gone. They are happy to show us the deed of sale of the house, another proof of respect and communal leaving. Yet we Jews have all left our houses and land, and it is difficult to reconcile their memories with that fact. It remains a difficult task albeit an important one, since as a historian I want to give full sense to my family's hasty exilic departures and nostalgic heritage returns. And I did fully appreciate that I can still visit my grandfather's home. Present-day Morocco is unique in the Arab-Muslim world in that it allows Jews of Moroccan descent to visit the country freely. This special relation, between the king and his Jewish subjects, is an exception in the Arab-Muslim world, a memory still cherished today.

According to some members of my family, the main disruptive forces in the displacement of these populations were French colonialism, and its false emancipatory promises, and Zionism, both messianic and modern. In Chapter 1, I detail the places where my family lived, retrace their steps thanks to the discussions I had with them despite their failing memories. Trying to make sense of their strategies and understand their motives left me with more questions than answers.

They left Morocco almost in a blink, attracted by the Zionist project and the prospect of building their own promised land. Their difficulties during the migration process, the rupture with half of their family members, the incredible losses they encountered, all that was (almost) forgotten when they set foot in Israel. Yet they did not encourage my parents to follow them, even though they were already stranded in Marseille, waiting for their visas to Israel. Instead, my parents went back to Meknès and decided to migrate to Canada in 1974. Feeling uprooted from their home country, they followed my mother's sister to Montreal. How did they arrive in Canada?

The second part of this volume covers Moroccan Jews' arrival in France and Canada, particularly in Montreal, where most of the French-speaking Moroccan Jews were eventually to settle. During post-colonial migrations, migrants reconstruct their identities and participate in community-building as they arrive in their new host country. Such is the case with North African migrations, which led Christians (who were for the most part, but not exclusively, repatriates and *Pieds-Noirs* from Algeria), Muslims, and Jews to leave colonial and national areas to regroup in towns in mainland France, then later in Canada and elsewhere in the West. Since these transnational migrants at first maintain the culture and traditions of their country of origin, the study should include their migration paths longitudinally, from their departure to their arrival. In this way, it becomes possible to identify the processes at work and to analyze closely the various reconfigurations that these migrations bring about. Chapter 3, written with Martin Messika, compares the occupations and marriage strategies developed by the migrants both in France and Canada. We found that when this relatively skilled population settled in urban areas, men had to spend several years in unskilled jobs before finding an appropriate occupation, while women were assigned to care for their families and children instead of entering the paid job market. At their arrival, very few women worked for a wage. For both women and men of this first cohort of migrants, marriage strategies were diverse. If most of them married other Moroccan Jews, one third of men in our cohort tended not to marry women from their country of origin, nor from their faith. Those men insisted nevertheless that their Catholic fiancée convert to Judaism, an indication of their strong identification to their own community of faith. As for this population's upward mobility, men fared better and succeeded more than women. For the second cohort of women, the acquisition of professional qualifications played a greater role than marriage in their social mobility. Overall, Moroccan Jews have integrated well and rapidly in both Paris and Montreal.

In Chapter 4, I continue examining their incorporation patterns in Montreal, a city with a strong multi-ethnic Jewish community. Their ability to become a thriving community was due to two main factors:

1. After the Holocaust, the Montreal-Jewish community's mobilization was crucial to open Canada's gates, which helped Jews migrate from Morocco. As they arrived in Montreal in the mid-sixties, Jewish institutions of relief helped them get established.
2. They also understood the crucial aspect of French language as an essential factor of integration. In a period of the Québécois' rising demand for sovereignty, aligning themselves with the francophone majority allowed them to set up their own French-language schools, institutions, and organizations, while most of the Jewish community still worked and thought in English.

If we understand how Montreal's Moroccan Jews achieved their economic and social gains, it is more difficult to analyze their collective identities and their sense of belonging. How do they make sense of their own migrations?

What Are the Stories We Tell?

The third section of this volume presents an even more subjective analysis of these questions. Digging into their many attachments, Martin Messika, Sara Cohen Fournier and I show in Chapter 5 how our informants perceived their migrations as they try to make sense of their lives. Analyzing their trajectories and the words they used to represent their exile allows us to understand the underlying traumas of their exiles. Yet, depending on the countries they left, the traumatic experience of their departure is recognized differently: It is seen as a forced migration for Jews from Machrek, while it is trivialized and considered voluntary for Jews for Maghreb. The importance of Jewish Immigrant Aid Services (JIAS) appears in all our informants' memories as an organization that facilitated their emigration to Canada, but very few acknowledge the fact that JIAS was rescuing them, because they were (potential) victims of antisemitism. If some of them ignored the fact that they were victims, they also sought to include their trajectories within a larger story of diaspora of the post-colonial type, one of continuous migration or transnational circulations. It allowed them to escape the status of victims, that of European Jews after the Shoah. By not confronting the events that shaped their lives as migrants, they ran the risk of failing to shake off an identity that is still one of survival and dislocation.

In a similar vein, I have tried, in chapters 6 and 7, to apply this dyad of forgetting and forging to my own trajectory, to highlight my father's memory. The Torah scroll that my family brought to Montreal is as much a remnant of our Moroccan past as a symbol of our desire to live as Jews in Canada.

Historiographical Framework

Scholarship on Moroccan Jews in Canada: Multidisciplinary, Multilingual, and Diasporic

Yolande Cohen and Stephanie Tara Schwartz

The study of Moroccan Jews in Canada is part of a broader and burgeoning field of Sephardic, Mizrahi, and Arab-Jewish studies (Cohen and Schwartz 2017). Within two decades of the establishment of the State of Israel in 1948, nearly the entire population of Jews (around 800,000) left their homes in North Africa, the Middle East, Iran, and Turkey and migrated to Israel, France, the United States, and Canada. In Jewish studies, the diverse histories of these Jews have generally been overshadowed by those of Ashkenazi (Eastern European) Jews. At the same time, Jewish histories in general are marginal to national histories, such as that of Morocco, though this has begun to change with works such as those by Kenbib (1994), Abitbol (2009), Miller (2013), and Kably (2013). With the vast migration of Moroccan Jews to Quebec after 1957, Canada became home to these migrants, as well as a crucial site for the study of Moroccan and Sephardic Jews.

The category of Jew is a notoriously difficult object of study due to its simultaneous and conflicting definitions as constituting a religious, ethnic, racial, national, and/or cultural group. According to Michael Brown (2007), in the period of binationalism from 1759 to the 1960s, "like French and Anglo-Canadians, Jews in Canada organized themselves as an ethnic group, a nationality, unlike American Jews, who organized as a religious group." This helps explain why the Federation of Zionist Societies, founded by Clarence de Sola, a Sephardic Jew in 1899, took hold as one of Canada's first national

Jewish organizations, until the Canadian Jewish Congress (CJC) formed in 1919; however, Richard Menkis (2011) demonstrated how the CJC preferred to define the Jewish community as a religious, rather than an ethnic, group during the 1963 Royal Commission on Bilingualism and Biculturalism (B&B Commission), which took place between 1963 and 1965. By dismissing the terms race and ethnicity as irrelevant to the inquiry and shifting the focus to culture, the CJC resisted the B&B Commission's designation of Jews under the category of "other ethnic groups" in contrast to Canada's "two founding races" (Haque 2012, 63–64).

Despite the fact that groups such as the left-wing secular Yiddishist Workmen's Circle wanted Jewish ethnic and national culture to be recognized (Menkis 2011, 289), Saul Hayes, the director of the CJC, ultimately preferred to follow the example of the United States and advocated for Canadian Jews to be recognized as a religious group rather than an ethnic group on par with Ukrainians and others. This tension has also been evident for social scientists in determining whether to count Jewish census data according to religion or ethnicity (Canada's long-form census included both possibilities before 2011), leading to the development of the Jewish Standard Definition, which includes Jewish ethnicity when no religion is indicated (Schnoor 2011).

In Canada and Quebec, the language/ethnicity/nation nexus has further complicated the category of Jews. The immigration of over 8,000 francophone Jews to Montreal from the 1960s to the 1980s during Quebec's modernization, secularization, and nationalization movements created a unique situation in the world (Miles 2012). Montreal's majority Jewish anglophone community, the largest in Canada at that time, was ultimately challenged to rethink its own self-definition and how it ran its institutions; Moroccan Jews were led to redefine themselves as Sephardim, and many non-Jewish Canadians and Quebecers were encouraged to rethink their stereotypes of Jews (once misunderstood as *juifs catholiques*). According to Miles (2012), this wave of immigration revealed the extent to which the religious ideal of Jewish unity clashed with the social fact of Sephardic and Ashkenazi ethnolinguistic subgroups that were perpetuated under Canadian multiculturalism and Quebec's commitment to being a francophone nation.

Quebec Jews historically have often been described as a third solitude, having a distinct ethnicity that developed between the competing nationalisms of English and French Canada. Education and public services in the province were divided along religious/linguistic lines and contributed to this triangulated development. In 1914, Yiddish was the third most spoken language in Quebec after French and English; by the 1960s, the Jewish community was largely anglophone. Jews had been designated Protestant under the province's confessional education system, and they attended English-language schools. As a result, in the 1970s, the majority of Montreal's 115,000 Jews, mostly of Ashkenazi background, were anglophone (Hayes 1977). The Quiet Revolution, which culminated with the election of the Parti Québécois (1976) and the adoption of the Charter of the French Language (1977), rattled the stability of Montreal Jews as anglophones in Quebec. This, combined with the declining numbers and the aging of the Jewish population, contributed to anxiety by Montreal Jewish leaders for their future in Quebec.

The CJC and Jewish Immigrant Aid Services (JIAS) (supported by the American Joint Distribution Committee) reached out to new immigration pools, including the Moroccan-Jewish community, as early as the 1950s. Spurred by the aftermath of the Shoah, they sought to rescue Jews from the Arab lands before it was too late, and at the same time to replenish the ranks of the Montreal-Jewish community, which was growing older and producing fewer children. Though Moroccan-Jewish migration to Canada began in 1957, it peaked in the years following Israel's 1967 war (the Six-Day War) and the violent repercussions it had on Jews in Morocco.

On a communal level, Moroccan Jews, arriving in Quebec during the Quiet Revolution, seized upon the opportunities afforded by a majority francophone population and the movement toward Francization to establish their own Jewish French-language schools (first with École Maïmonide, then École Sépharade and Académie Yahvné), organizations (i.e., Communauté sépharade du Québec [CSQ], Centre communautaire juif, Département francophone du Y, Hillel français), and a distinct identity apart from the Ashkenazim. We have focused on francophone Moroccans in Quebec, but there are also Spanish-speaking Moroccan-Jewish communities in Montreal and Toronto who are even further marginalized in the literature.

Moroccan Jews organized themselves under the rubric of the Association sépharade francophone (ASF), creating a unique Sephardic identity that gathered a loose network of non-Ashkenazim, including Iraqis, Egyptians, and others. Despite these efforts to forge independent Sephardic institutions, Moroccan Jews remained under the towering power of Ashkenazi organizations (Lasry and Tapia 1989; Tulchinsky 2008, 453–456). The clash between Ashkenazim and Sephardim proved to be one of the most enduring misunderstandings that still hovers over the Jewish community of Montreal. The conflict between these groups in Canada should be viewed in relation to the global situation of displaced Moroccan Jews vying to forge diaspora networks around Sephardic or Mizrahi identities. It is from this background that we can begin to explore the historiography of Moroccan Jews in Canada as an essentially diasporic one.

Immigration and Integration

The first academic literature on Moroccan Jews appeared in the late 1960s, mostly in English by faculty and students at McGill University's School of Social Work, connected to the JIAS. These writings focus on understanding family life (Amber and Lipper 1968), economic adjustment of North African immigrants (Moldofsky 1968), immigration (Berman, Nahmiash, and Osmer 1970), and integration (Batshaw and Low 1971). The question of immigrant adjustment stands out in these studies, the goal being to determine how to best integrate these Jewish immigrants with different languages, religious practices, and backgrounds into Canada and the established Jewish community. Together with the question of language and demography (Légaré 1965), there was also a concern with the identification of these new immigrants to their Jewishness, Moroccanness, or Frenchness.

Meanwhile, as early as 1975, Moroccan Jews themselves began to publish academic papers and dissertations about their community, with the clear intention of establishing their distinct (francophone) identity. Jean-Claude Lasry, a long-time activist and president of the ASF from 1972 to 1974, published articles on Moroccan Jewish immigration and mental health in *Social Psychiatry* (1977) and *International Review of Applied Psychology* (1980). In 1976, Esther Benaïm completed her PhD thesis on the integration of Moroccan Jews in Canada under the supervision of Moroccan-Jewish scholar Doris Bensimon Donath in Paris. Benaïm argued that the French language permitted the Sephardim in Quebec to distinguish themselves from the Ashkenazim, who dominated and controlled community spaces in Montreal (Cohen and Guerry 2011, 295). She wrote about the Moroccan Jews of Quebec as part of the Jewish diaspora (Benaïm 1977) and on the paradox of being a Jew and becoming

Sephardic in Quebec (Benaïm 1979). In 1979, Fernand G. Filion completed his PhD thesis also on the Sephardic-Jewish community of Quebec and its institutionalization. While previous studies had specified North African or Moroccan communities, Filion used the term *communauté sépharade*, reflecting the change in community self-representation with the formation of the CSQ (Communauté sépharade du Québec) in 1976.

This early writing on Moroccan Jews in Montreal was focused on the integration of Moroccan-Jewish immigrants into Quebec and into a Jewish diaspora on a psychological or ethnohistorical level (Bordes-Benayoun and Schnapper 2006). These articles were explicitly transnational—they were connected to both Moroccan and Jewish diasporas and less concerned with a Canadian national framework. While this can likely be explained by the relatively recent immigration of Moroccan Jews to Canada, these works took place in a particular context. The 1970s were a potent time politically for Moroccan Jews in Israel, which had repercussions for how they were being studied in Montreal and Paris. Mizrahim (Eastern or Oriental Jews from North Africa and the Middle East) were fighting against the second-class treatment they had been receiving since their migration to Israel. Concern for the treatment of Moroccan Jews under the Ashkenazi regime became a global concern. Ongoing conflict in the Middle East between Israel, Palestine, and surrounding Arab states led some to become very involved in peace initiatives.

Benaïm, for example, was active in both the CSQ in Montreal and the international group Identité et dialogue, headed by André Azoulay, which aimed to promote Sephardic-Jewish history and to build intercultural dialogue, especially between Arabs and Jews. It reaffirmed the Arab identity of Moroccan Jews, as well as their proximity with Israel, pitching them as emissaries of peace in the Arab-Israeli conflict. This was also the aim of the conference organized by the group in Paris in December 1978 and its published proceedings, *Juifs du Maroc : identité et dialogue* (1980). With representatives from Canada, France, Morocco, and Israel, the conference saw the liminal group of Moroccan Jews in Israel, dominated by Ashkenazi authorities and sharing elements of language and culture with Palestinians, as potential mediators for establishing an alternative path to peace in the Middle East. The conference helped create a network of academic and community activists who started to work on the project of strengthening the Moroccans' position in international Jewish organizations (with the creation of the

World Sephardi Federation), as well as upgrading the status of the Moroccan-Jewish population in Israel.

In the context of the political upheavals in both Canada and Israel during this period, there is evidence that Moroccan Jews were looking to international solidarity movements rather than to the Canadian national framework. Books and articles on Canadian Jews more generally tended to focus on biographies of individuals, such as the opera singer Pauline Donalda (Brotman 1975) or efforts like that of David Rome's (1974, 1975) archival compilations to systematically document the key issues of Canadian-Jewish history. The seed of a comprehensive Canadian-Jewish studies field was just beginning to be planted, while writings on Moroccan Jews were already transnational and diasporic due to the nature of the community's numerous displacements and its relatively recent immigration. In the political context of the 1980s, studies on Moroccan Jews would remain peripheral to the effort to write Canadian-Jewish history, but bridges had begun to be built across the lines of the language divide.

Recognition and Rapprochement

The 1980s saw the publication of the first academic monographs on Jews and Canada. First was Abella and Troper's (1982) groundbreaking *None Is Too Many*, which revealed Canada's antisemitic immigration policy toward Jews during the 1930s and 1940s. Michael Brown's (1987) *Jew or Juif? Jews, French Canadians, and Anglo-Canadians, 1759–1914* was the first book to analyze Quebec's Jewish community as a third solitude; this was followed shortly by Michael Greenstein's (1989) *Third Solitude: Tradition and Discontinuity in Jewish-Canadian Literature*. Brown ponders why Jews in Quebec identified so strongly with English Canada rather than with French Quebec. The answer to this question, he argues, lies within the defining period of 1759–1914, when the Jewish community of Montreal established itself and its allegiances, which would influence communal relations into the tense political climate of the 1980s. Their own version of nationalism—Zionism, rather than Canadian or Quebec nationalism—united Canadian Jews during this early period through the Federation of Zionist Societies in Canada. According to Brown (1987), the high rate of intermarriage between North African Jews and French Canadians in the 1960s signalled a potential change: that French Canada had become more welcoming to Jews in general.

In contrast to anglophone studies of Canadian Jews that stressed Jewish distinctiveness from other national communities within the framework of multiculturalism, francophone Quebec scholars were more concerned with rapprochement, an attempt to build bridges between Jews and French Québécois under Quebec's new national project. For example, Anctil and Caldwell (1984) published the edited collection *Juifs et réalités juives au Québec* under the rubric of Montreal's Institut québécois de recherche sur la culture. The authors' aim was to make the history and sociology of Quebec's ethnocultural minorities more accessible to the Québécois "de vieille souche." They did this by emphasizing the *Québécois* identity of Quebec Jews (in contrast to studies of the Jewish community, which had been predominantly from a Canadian perspective) and by making links between Jewish and francophone Québécois experiences of oppression and communal strategies in the diaspora. Langlais and Rome's (1986) book *Juifs et Québécois français* is another attempt at ameliorating relations between Jews and French Canadians during this period of encounters with the other while integrating Jewish experiences within a Quebec national narrative. This book, too, focuses on the Ashkenazi-Jewish community with only a brief section on the "Arrival of French-Speaking Jews," whom the authors believe can help bridge the gap between anglophone Jews and French Québécois. These outreach and collaborative endeavours occurred during the decade of a mass exodus of anglophone Jews out of Montreal and Quebec. It is surprising, however, that both works fail to incorporate more fully the voices of Moroccan-Jewish scholars, who were becoming increasingly active in telling their own histories.

Between the competing discourses of anglophone Jews trying to articulate a Canadian-Jewish history and French Québécois hoping to fold Jews into a Quebec national narrative, Moroccan-Jewish scholars were mainly concerned by this displaced population's fate, stressing the continuity of its diasporic relations to Morocco and Israel. Mikhaël Elbaz, anthropologist at Laval University, conducted an important study on the plight of Moroccan Jews in Israel. Through his work on generational changes in the Moroccan-Jewish population in Montreal, Quebec, and Israel, Elbaz (1986, 1989, 1993) observed a sharp change within the younger group, documenting the religious turn that took place in the 1980s. For Elbaz, the second generation's quest for a stable identity had led many in the younger generation of Moroccan Jews toward a more orthodox Judaism, fuelled by Ashkenazi rabbis, and against the secularism of their parents. For this group, religious revival and the adoption of Ashkenazi orthodoxy was the way to integrate into Israeli and Canadian societies. For the older group, for which Jean-Claude Lasry seems to be the spokesperson, secularism and Sephardism were the essential pillars of identity. Striving to assess their difference, whether in the languages they spoke, their cultural habits, or religious traditions, Lasry's works focused on the difference of the Moroccan-Jewish community from both Canadian and Quebec nations. The inclusion of Lasry's (1981) article "A Francophone Diaspora in Quebec" in the English-language anthology *The Canadian Jewish Mosaic*, edited by Morton Weinfeld, William Shaffir, and Irwin Cotler, was a first attempt to bridge anglophone and francophone Jewish scholarship under the rubric of Canadian-Jewish studies. The article nevertheless stressed the language divide, as well as the differences between Sephardi and Ashkenazi Jews.

Concerned with the questions raised by the massive displacement of their community, Berdugo-Cohen, Cohen, and Lévy (1987) and André Elbaz (1988) documented Moroccan Jews' experiences of migration from sociological and historical frameworks. They were the first to look at autobiography and oral history as methods for exploring the perceptions of three generations of Moroccan-Jewish immigrants, producing a trove of oral archives that documented their memories of migration and exile. Influenced by the growing interest in oral history as a way to give a voice to invisible or marginalized minorities (Draper and Karlinsky 1986), the book *Juifs marocains à Montréal* (Berdugo-Cohen, Cohen and Lévy 1987) presents the different themes that structured the migrants' experiences and memories of migration. Their life stories stressed the first generation's nostalgia for, as well as their silence about, the causes of their migrations (Cohen 2011). Also outlined are the hectic paths those migrants took before arriving in Canada, their transitions through different locations, and their unending circulations. Oral testimonies—valuable first-hand accounts of Moroccan-Jewish life and migration—offered ample individual reflections on these migrations (Cohen and Messika 2012; Cohen, Messika, and Cohen Fournier 2015). Sharing those memories allowed the participants to feel an agency in their lives, as it gave a voice to those otherwise silenced. Focusing on the migrant's perceptions of their own lives, the study shows their ambivalences and various attachments, their nostalgic memories, and their losses.

On another side of the spectrum, Lasry and Tapia (1989), in their edited volume *Les Juifs du Maghreb: diasporas contemporaines*, contextualized

Maghrebi-Jewish experiences in terms of diaspora. The sociological bent of the book prioritizes quantitative and descriptive analysis but lacks a complex theory of ethnicity or diaspora to back up the studies, even as it insists upon such a framework for contemplating the experiences of Moroccan Jews. These works by Moroccan-Jewish authors demonstrated a unique approach to scholarship on Canadian Jews and a means of announcing their inclusion in scholarship on Jews in Canada and Quebec. At the same time, Ashkenazi-Jewish scholars, such as the performer and ethnomusicologist Judith Cohen, began to take a more active interest in the study of Moroccan-Jewish culture. Cohen (1982, 1989a, 1989b) published several articles on Judeo-Spanish traditional song, beginning to link Moroccan Jews' culture and music in Montreal and Toronto.

Multiculturalism, Interculturalism, and the Production of Ethnicity

Shifting into the 1990s, Canadian-Jewish studies highlighted the key themes of antisemitism (Davies 1992) and multiculturalism (Adelman and Simpson 1996) for articulating a national Jewish consciousness. We see the first large-scale Canadian-Jewish histories in Gerald Tulchinsky's (1992, 1998) *Taking Root: The Origins of the Canadian Jewish Community* and *Branching Out: The Transformations of the Canadian Jewish Community*. In his preface to *Taking Root*, Tulchinsky argues that the Canadian-Jewish community developed differently from American Jewry in the context of a range of unique conditions, from the duality of its national personality (a conflict between French and English) to distinct immigration, economic, and urban-growth patterns. The community that evolved was

> more traditional, more superficially unified, and more culturally homogenous than that of our U.S. cousins. While American Jewry yearned for integration into the mainstream of the great republic, Canadians strove to express their Jewishness in a country that had no coherent self-definition—except perhaps the solitudes of duality, isolation, northernness, and borrowed glory.

Tulchinsky's two-book project, published initially in 1992 and reissued in 1998 (the two volumes were updated and combined into one book in 2008), was the first, comprehensive history of Canada's Jews, stretching from St. John's to Victoria, beginning with the settlement of Jews in Quebec in the 1760s and continuing to the time of writing. His work was emblematic of a general nation-building project by Canadians, which was at its peak in the 1990s, to define themselves against the cultural domination of their national neighbour to the south. As Koffman (2013) writes, this was the beginning of Canadian-Jewish studies (CJS) as a "bona fide" field. In 1993, the Canadian Jewish Historical Society (established in the 1970s) became the Association for Canadian Jewish Studies (ACJS), and the organization's journal changed its name to *Canadian Jewish Studies*. Under its new mandate, ACJS broadened its scope from a focus on history to also include sociology, literary studies, and political science. By 1999, Brown, Menkis, Schlesinger, and Schoenfeld (1999–2000) had recorded over 1,600 books and articles on Canadian Jews from the fields of history, political science, economics, anthropology, sociology, women's studies, literature, and others. While CJS was defining itself in contrast to studies in the United States, however, Jewish pluralism in itself was something of an afterthought. The specificity of the still rather recent migration of North African Jews was perceived as relatively irrelevant to the production of a national ethnic group, which was the aim of Brym, Shaffir, and Weinfeld's (1993) edited volume *The Jews in Canada*. The inclusion of Lasry's (1983) article "Sephardim and Ashkenazim in Montréal" in the seventh and final section of the book, entitled "Minorities," along with articles about Russian Jews in Toronto, Jewish survival in small communities in Canada, Jewish poverty and Aliyah, and return migration, bore witness to this. Like Lasry's 1981 contribution to *The Canadian Jewish Mosaic Anthology*, this offered another example of the editors' will to integrate Moroccan Jews into a comprehensive CJS perspective. Lasry's insistence on the radical difference between Ashkenazim and Sephardim fed into the multiculturalist discourse, yet the framing of his article within the overall work declared that Jewish diversity was a minor issue compared to those such as antisemitism. Multiculturalism was useful for anglophone Jews trying to construct a unified ethnic voice vis-à-vis English and French Canada but not for promoting multicultural Jewish identities as such (Byers and Schwartz 2013).

For Moroccan-Jewish scholars, multiculturalism offered an opportunity. Lévy and Cohen's (1992) *Itinéraires sépharades : l'odyssée des Juifs sépharades de l'Inquisition à nos jours* aimed at recapturing Moroccan-Jewish history within its multi-secular Sephardic roots. Lévy and Cohen also oversaw the production of a multimedia CD-ROM

Juifs marocains : traditions et modernité (2000), which featured sections on Moroccan-Jewish music, religious traditions and cantillation, culture, and culinary tastes, and a biographical dictionary containing more than 2,000 names. Written and published in French, these works signalled the wills of their authors to reassess the existence of a world and culture that was waning under their eyes; at the same time, they established links with the communities in the diaspora, especially in Montreal. This attempt at building a common Sephardi identity was done within the multicultural lens.

During this period, scholarship on Moroccan Jews increasingly demonstrated the richness of Moroccan-Jewish diversity and cultural production as distinct from that of Ashkenazi Jews. Suzanne Myers Sawa (1991) published an article in *Canadian Folk Music Journal* on the difficulties faced by the Jewish Marrakesh-born, Canadian-trained, Middle Eastern dancer Dahlia Obadia. Lucette Heller-Goldenberg (1997) wrote about Quebec as a site where Moroccan-Jewish culture, threatened by the near-dissolution of Moroccan-Jewish life in Morocco, was preserved through its literary works. With the end of mass Moroccan-Jewish migration after 1980, issues of integration and institutional development were discussed in works by Taïeb-Carlen (1996) and Cohen and Lévy (1998). In the 1990s, multiculturalism was used as a tool by Moroccan Jews to escape the religious minority status (and its related antisemitism) and to enter the broader Canadian and Quebec citizenry through its openness to ethnic minorities in this period. They succeeded in creating their own sub-ethnic group within the Jewish community with its distinct Sephardic identity. These publications, mainly produced by Moroccan-Jewish scholars attuned to the need to grasp their own history, attest also to the co-construction of a subfield within Jewish studies, as well as North African and Middle Eastern studies. Paradoxically, both Canadian multiculturalism and Quebec interculturalism helped prompt this ethnic turn.

Memory, Identity, and Religion

The trend toward the recognition of the plurality of ethnic voices became even more apparent in the following decade. With the growth of works on identity and memory in social sciences and the humanities, Jewish subjects also gained traction in a number of different ways, including the reassessment of religion as the basis for community belonging. Since 2000, there has been an explosion in scholarship on Canadian and Quebec Jews in general, doubling from the production in the 1980s and 1990s. Koffman (2013) counted over seven hundred articles on Canadian-Jewish subjects produced between 1999 and 2013, with history as the primary disciplinary approach (at 25 percent). He observed further that most of these articles were published in Jewish studies journals, with very few in Canadian studies journals, and were multidisciplinary rather than interdisciplinary. There was a move toward greater Jewish diversity in works such as Menkis and Ravvin's (2004) *The Canadian Jewish Studies Reader*. Unlike in previous anthologies organized chronologically, Janice Rosen's essay "Moroccan Jewish Saint Veneration: From the Maghreb to Montreal" appeared among the first chapters in the volume, which were organized thematically. This reflected a growing trend of the diversification of CJS, with Shaffir's (2001, 2002) writing on Hassidim, Bialystok's (2000) work on the impact of the Holocaust on the Canadian-Jewish community, and articles by Wolfman (2002) and Schnoor (2006) and a PhD dissertation by Lash (2007) concerning gay and lesbian Canadian-Jewish identities.

Indeed, the cultural turn in the humanities and social sciences in the United States offered a new avenue for integrating Jewish cultures and experiences in national and transnational settings (Biale 2002). It encouraged the exploration of a large array of languages and diverse cultures and experiences of Sephardic Jews. Their lives under colonial rule, whether French, British, Spanish, Portuguese, or Italian, made theirs a unique place to explore post-colonial settings and changes (Valensi 2002). A deeper understanding of the larger culture of Jews in Muslim lands can still emerge from these studies since their cultural boundaries are more pervasive than the national ones.

The cultural turn also occurred internationally with the development of multidisciplinary Sephardic studies. The question of how the Jews lived/survived/strived in Muslim lands offered a new means of analyzing their cultures, practices, and choices of where to migrate. Their languages, habits, foodways, and religious practices were scrutinized in relation to their traditional and new environments (Cohen, Messika, and Cohen Fournier 2015). Informed by a wealth of works on Moroccan Jews produced by historians in Israel (Abitbol 2009), France (Abécassis et al. 2012), and the United States (Schroeter 2002, 2008), a new consideration grew around the importance of establishing a clear historical documentation of these people's fate after the Second World War. The role of transnational Jewish organizations (such as the

American Jewish Joint Distribution Committee), as well as the role of the Israeli immigration offices (such as the Jewish Agency), was central to that historical claim (Cohen and Messika 2012). Maud Mandel's (2014) study shows that international Jewish organizations created a category of "Juifs d'Afrique du Nord," bringing attention and specific public policies to the difficulties they encountered in settling in France, as one example.

There is also a move toward diversity in Sephardic publications. In literary studies, for example, Heller-Goldenberg (2004) and Redouane (2004) explore, respectively, Moroccan and Sephardic literature. We can also observe a rise of literary scholars taking interest in the works of Iraqi-Jewish writer Naim Kattan and Egyptian-Jewish writer Victor Teboul (Sadock 2006; Dahab 2009); as well, Jean-Luc Bédard (2005, 2007) and Kelly Amanda Train (2008), both in the field of sociology, have contributed PhD theses and scholarly publications on Sephardim.

It is worth highlighting here the conference and subsequent publication *Identités sépharades et modernité*, edited by Jean-Claude Lasry, Joseph Lévy, and Yolande Cohen (2007). The conference's organizers attempted to stress the importance of listening to other voices in the Jewish community that were expressing themselves in the academy and, more broadly, in intellectual circles.

Jean-Luc Bédard's (2007, 178) article in the previously mentioned volume followed Mikhaël Elbaz (1993) in arguing that re-diasporisation—a superimposition of a second exile (from Morocco) on the classic diasporic relationship with Israel—is a major factor in the collective memory of Moroccan Jews living in Montreal. The community had to negotiate their relationship between here and there, their homeland (Morocco), or nostalgia for, and the impossibility or undesirability of return. Other important factors for the community included the ambiguity of their relationship to French culture, which served to link them to modernity in Morocco; their identification with new localities in North America, where, for example, the ethnonym Sephardic was adopted; and the process of *rejudaisation*. For some Moroccan-Jewish youth, religiosity accompanied the reconstruction of the memory of origins in Morocco. Families and individuals began to distance themselves from each other and from the institutionalized community, with the Communauté sépharade unifiée du Québec (CSUQ) linking itself more strongly to religion. The creation of schools (such as L'Académie Yéchiva Yavné) on the model of Ashkenazi orthodoxy had been at the centre of a heated debate within CSUQ itself. On one side, the first generation of community leaders considered themselves to be secular Jews, eager to defend their view of their community as built on an ethnocultural basis; on the other, a second generation of community leaders now strove to defend a *rejudaisation* of the community.

Claude Tapia's (2007) article in the *Identités sépharades et modernité* volume situated Sephardism specifically within the realm of *francité*. This article stood in contrast to works of other scholars such as Ella Shohat (2002), who called for Mizrahi studies that question the Mizrahi subaltern position in Israel and unravel both the abuses faced by those populations in Israel, as well as the mythologies that enabled it. These publications reflected the extent to which the study of Moroccan Jews in Canada continues to require a multinational approach, reflecting the influence of international concerns for a diasporic population.

The Sephardic-Jewish community of Quebec has itself continued to change over time, shifting its focal point further from Morocco and closer to France and Israel, as is evident from analyses of its community newspaper *La voix sépharade* (LVS) (Manac'h 2006). The paper, at first, devoted little attention to Canadian and Québécois topics. A few decades later, the CSUQ leadership left its secularist ambition to embrace all expressions of religion, as well as an overtly Zionist stance during the difficult times Israel was going through. Not that these positions were non-existent before, but they were covered by a concern to establish a specific space for the community. The power struggle of the first group of young and not-so-young male community leaders with their Ashkenazi counterparts that had been occurring since the 1960s receded behind the need to gather all forces around Israel in the 1980s. Another younger generation of Moroccan-Jewish community leaders came to see this objective, together with a religious stance, as central to its activity; at least, this is how we can understand it through the changing directions of LVS articles (Manac'h 2006).

Since 2010, publications about and by Moroccan Jews in Canada have continued to increase. From David Bensoussan's (2010) edited collections on Sephardic writers to Yolande Cohen's (2010, 2011, 2015) work on migration and memory; Mechtild Gilzmer's (2010) articles on Sephardic literature in Quebec; Kelly Amanda Train's (2013) work on North African Jewish experiences in Toronto; Jessica Roda's (2015) article on Montreal's Festival Sefarad; and Martin Messika's (2015) thesis on the politics of integration, compared in Canada and France, the growth of a rich literature has been demonstrated in recent years. These authors continue to further trends begun in the 1990s and 2000s toward the diversification of literature on Moroccan Jews. From the focus on integration and immigration in the 1960s and 1970s, the study of Moroccan Jews in Canada has shifted to a study of Moroccan Jews as individuals and comprising multiple communities in their own right and in relation to communities beyond national frameworks. The example of Moroccan-Jewish studies in Canada demonstrates the particularities of studying multilingual, religious, and ethnic minorities beyond the master national narratives of Canada and Quebec. Moroccan Jews, because of their ongoing diasporic connections with Morocco, France, Israel, and the United States, and because of their internal diversity of language—French, Spanish, Judeo-Arabic—resist a single disciplinary lens, as do their religion and cultures. As such, this scholarship provides an example to Canadian studies: that they should further strive to reach across francophone and anglophone scholarship and partake in studies on Canadians from beyond a Canadian studies framework.

In anglophone publications, Canada-US comparisons have often been made in efforts to write about Jewish experience in Canada as a whole. It is striking that Sephardic studies, in contrast, has been taken up in journals dedicated to francophone studies rather than Jewish studies specifically. France is a more frequent frame of reference for Sephardic studies and was long before the rise of Sephardic studies in the United States. Works on Sephardim thus reached different audiences than articles in anglophone Canadian-Jewish studies. We might consider these as being more diasporic in reach—not limited to a single national framework, but instead jumping between multiple homelands, reflecting the experiences of Moroccan Jews. In France, too, Sephardic studies had trouble finding its place. This could be attributed to the ways in which Franco-Judaism defined itself first as French and then as Jewish. Unlike in France, however, where Franco-Judaism has defined the field of Jewish studies for the last century, we cannot find in Canada the same urge to establish what it is to be a Canadian Jew.

Scholarship on Moroccan Jews in Canada reveals an ambivalent relationship between a national and diasporic framework for making sense of Jewish experiences in Canada and Quebec. On one hand, the nationalist framework makes the case for paying attention to the unique experiences of Jews in Canada as opposed to other national or geographic contexts and encourages its scholarly production. On the other hand, the nationalist framework will never satisfy the complexities of Jewishness between the two competing national contexts in

Canada—and the diasporic networks maintained by groups such as the Moroccans with France, Israel, and the United States. At best, the national framework is a starting point for an ongoing conversation about Jewish history as part of a transnational network, but it should not be its ending point. This extends to Jewish studies as whole, as the expansion of Sephardic and Mizrahi studies continues to challenge the field.

PART I

The Jews of Morocco and Their Departures

CHAPTER 1

From Synagogue to Mosque: My Grandfather's House in the Old Mellah of Meknès

Yolande Cohen and Noureddine Harrami

Emanuela Trevisan Semi is the inspiration for this chapter.[1] She was the one who encouraged me to visit my grandfather's house in Meknès, came with me for this very emotional return to my family's birthplace, kept the pictures we took there and sent them back to me when I lost them, and finally pushed me to realize this project, which formed the background for this presentation within a larger project. The (nostalgic) emotion and several not-so-accidental encounters at a colloquium in Meknès, organized by Noureddine Harrami, were all related to Emanuela's seminal anthropological works in Meknès (Trevisan and Hatimi 2015).

---

[1] Yolande Cohen and Noureddine Harrami, "From Synagogue to Mosque: My Grandfather's House in the Old Mellah of Meknes," in *Homelands and Diasporas: Perspectives on Jewish Culture in the Mediterranean and Beyond*, ed. Dario Miccoli, Marcella Simoni, and Giorgia Foscarini (Newcastle upon Tyne: Cambridge Scholars Publishing, 2018), 26–40. This chapter was first presented as a paper at the conference "The Ghetto Reconsidered: Ethnic and Minority Quarters in Texts and Images," Ca' Foscari University, Venice, 2–3 March 2016. The paper was then reworked and Yolande Cohen presented it as the keynote address at the Israeli Anthropological Association in Tiberias, Israel, in May 2016. We wish to thank Harvey Goldberg for his kind remarks and the very professional translation from French to English by Jackie Feldman. Our thanks also go to Steven Lapidus and to the editors for their thoughtful comments.

Noureddine and I decided to analyze my grandfather's legacy from a dual perspective for this chapter: Taking the historical research on the house of my grandfather as its starting point, we reflect on several ethnological aspects of Jewish life in the *mellah* of Meknès. The period covered by the inquiry starts in 1930, when my grandfather bought the house in the height of the French protectorate. Sold by my uncle in 1969, the synagogue housed in the house (*slat* [in Judeo-Arabic, lit. "synagogue"] Rabbi Smea't ya) is transformed into a small mosque, the only one in the ancient *mellah* at the time. Then the commemoration of the house situated in the old *mellah*, and of its Jewish inhabitants, became the object of the fieldwork conducted recently by Noureddine in Meknès.

Noureddine conducted interviews with witnesses to the process of transformation of the synagogue into a mosque and documented the memories of this house of prayer, which was transferred from Jews to Muslims, as well as its significance in the contemporary space. My contribution was to verify several elements of family history and its transmission in the present, in an attempt to compose a historical, albeit subjective, narrative. Thus, with our two voices, we seek to explore the informal system of communication between Jews and Muslims, past and present, "between the two riverbanks of colonization" (Balhoul 1983), which are at the heart of this story, as well as the conflicts over the suppression of memory that it evokes.

The role of this house provides a case study, which sheds light on the dynamics of exchange among Jews and Muslims at two moments in their shared history, during and after colonization. The *mellahs* are separate spaces in certain cities, in which the Jewish populations of Morocco lived, but were also, as Daniel Schroeter and Emily Gottreich (2011) noted, places of interaction between Jews and Muslims. They were an integral part of the urban fabric and constituted liminal spaces (Gottreich 2007), from which Jews could leave (to work in the *suq*, market), while Muslims could enter to carry out their various activities, both economic and religious (such as visiting pilgrimage sites), as well as for entertainment, such as drinking alcohol.

The term used to designate such Jewish quarters varied from place to place: They were called *mellahs* in Morocco and *harat* (quarters) in Tunisia and in Egypt. In Morocco, the first *mellah* was created in Fès in 1438, whereas the *mellah* of Meknès was established in 1675, following the designation of the city as capital under Sultan Moulay Isma'il. The Jewish community of Meknès, which was of great importance, had significant influence in the religious domain, and was even called "Little Jerusalem." In response to the poor conditions of life in the *mellah*, a new *mellah* was built beginning in 1924. The first houses of the new *mellah* were erected alongside the old *mellah*, and one of the first synagogues was founded in 1926.

Colonization as well as urban development of the early twentieth century engendered changes in Jewish residential patterns. This was the case in Tangiers, as studied by Susan Gilson Miller, who demonstrated that, notwithstanding the concentration of synagogues in the Beni Ider quarter, the area was not defined as a Jewish quarter. The transformation of the city of Tangiers, in the early twentieth century, was linked to the influx of capital and the development of new construction, including the construction of new dwellings for the elite (Miller 2011, 128–149). Moreover, the development of new cities made the traditional structure of the *mellah* obsolete. It resulted in the exodus of the wealthier Jews to the new Europeanized cities, and, consequently, a deterioration of the Jewish quarters along with an influx of non-Jewish populations to those areas. Through our study of the house of Eliezer Berdugo and the changes in the names of sites in Meknès, we seek to investigate the mechanisms of appropriation of Jewish-Moroccan urban space and the suppression of the Jewish memory of those quarters.

The Grandfather: Eliezer Berdugo, a Traditional Local Personage

I know nothing of him, or almost nothing. His photo dominated my mother's room, and after many changes of residence, it wound up in my house in Montreal. I had to explain to my children that the austere gaze of this proud-looking man in the picture was that of my maternal grandfather. My mother carried this photo with her wherever she lived, and I kept it in memory of her. I still have it, because I throw nothing out; it has its place in my room, until I decide what to do with it. I have had this photo for over 40 years, this photo that I do not like, because there is no other memory attached to it, except perhaps the sadness of my mother when she spoke of her father, who died prematurely on the eve of her wedding in 1948.

Eliezer Berdugo was a notable in the Jewish community of Meknès, who served as judge of the rabbinical court and also mediated inter-communal disputes. Owner of a soap factory in Berrima (a neighbourhood located between the old *mellah* and Sakkakine in the Old City), he also received income from properties he owned in the region of Meknès, and was, among other things, in charge of selling wheat and other grains brought to him by farmers or other agriculturalists. The papers documenting the sale of the house indicate that he was the owner of seven shops, which abutted his house in the old *mellah*. He was the kind of notable described so well by Susan Miller, who wrote of merchants active in Tangiers at the turn of the twentieth century, but unlike the bazaar salesmen of the *mellah* of Sefrou described by Lawrence Rosen (Miller 2011; Rosen 1984).

Thus, he was a well-to-do owner of both agricultural lands and several shops. In 1930, he acquired a large aristocratic residence in the old *mellah*, purchased, according to family history, from another Jew, named Benabou, who lived in Rabat and wanted to sell off his second house. Along with my grandfather came a small group of around fifteen families who had lived in the old *mellah* for several generations—the families Ohana, Toledano, Boussidan, Hassine, and others, who had made it in the wholesale business of basic commodities like grain, oil, sugar, and—in his case—*beldi* (local) soap. They distinguished themselves by their clothes (traditional *djellaba* and *tarboosh* at home and European suits at work and in public), their aristocratic houses, and their status as community leaders. Living in the old *mellah*, they were both at a distance from non-Jews, separated by walls of religious difference while maintaining relations with all, both outside the walls of the *mellah* and during their working hours. Their status as notables was expressed in numerous ways, both symbolic and real. In the *mellah* their prominence was recognized through their family names, a lineage of well-known families of *hakhamim* (rabbis, religious scholars, lit.: "wise men"), which often entitled them to become community leaders. Members of these families also built or moved to bigger houses in this period, lending a new significance to housing as a status symbol under the French regime. For my grandfather too, moving into this patrician house was certainly a sign of wanting to acquire this form of capital. Keeping his family in the old *mellah*, while other Jews had already moved to the new *mellah* or even the Ville Nouvelle, signalled on the other hand his attachment to the traditional view of being notable, supported by an uncontested paternalism and an accepted hierarchy of class and gender.

The cooperation among ethno-religious elites within different cultural communities was commonplace and is affirmed in numerous studies. In the particular case of my grandfather, however, it remained beyond the influence of the French. Thus, he did not become, as many Jews at the time did, Westernized or Europeanized (Tsur 1995). He was neither an *évolué* (enlightened) nor a *protégé* (protected) (Kenbib 1996). Like the Moroccan subjects of the French protectorate, he spoke only Arabic and wrote only in Judeo-Arabic. Judeo-Arabic, as a written and spoken language, was reduced to the status of a dialect by French linguists in 1930, even though it was the *lingua franca* of the Jews of the Maghreb (Kosansky 2016). Thus, my grandfather was attached to an ancient tradition, one that had been totally transformed by French modernity. By *choosing* to remain in the old *mellah*, he rooted himself in a place that was undergoing complete transformation. For him, this space remained a place of commerce and inter-religious exchange. Having his family and businesses alongside the artisans and traders who lived in these very narrow alleys and these houses all crowded together, he was an integral part of this ancient Jewish community with its many synagogues. The purchase of the house in 1930 marked his involvement and the engagement of this small group of notables in relation to their surroundings—both separate and symbiotic. Much research has characterized these spaces as ghettos—paradoxical or ambiguous spaces enclosing the Jews, yet open to commerce. In the case of the old *mellah* of Meknès, we witness intense convivial interpersonal relationships between Jews and Muslims in daily life, alongside a respect for strict rules of separation in the spaces they lived in, as regulated by the laws of *Dhimma* (restricting their rights while authorizing their cult).

But what occurred to these relations in post-colonial Morocco? Some answers may be found in the sale documents of the house and the built-up areas, while others are provided by analyzing the transformations of the quarter and its street names.

The Berdugo House: From Synagogue to Mosque

The house is located at 25, Derb al Ghoufrane. At the time, the street was called Slaouats (Synagogues Street), as is attested in the old bill of sale. The buyer was Moulay Hachem ben El Mahdi ben Mohamad El Alaoui Slimani. According to his son Ahmed, the house was purchased in 1965, though the bill of sale is dated 8 October 1969. The sale was not done hastily and under pressure, as was the case with many Jewish properties both in the *mellah* and elsewhere, when, in the years of mass migration to Israel, Jewish properties were sold at much reduced prices. This explains the price of 27,500 dirhams, or 5,400 dollars, which was considered as high at the time. The house has four storeys. The ground floor housed a synagogue (called a *masjid*, a place of prayer, in the bill of sale) and seven shops. The apartment on the second floor is today the residence of Ahmed, the son of Moulay Hachem. With respect to the circumstances surrounding the purchase, Ahmed told us that his father learned from a merchant in the quarter that "Ouled (the son of) Berdugo was looking to sell." Ahmed added that his grandfather knew Eliezer Berdugo, further evidence of cross-cultural exchange.

The seventeen synagogues of the *mellah* experienced a variety of destinies. Some fell into ruin, while others were transformed into residences. S'lat Berdugo (Synagogue Berdugo), as it was called by many residents, was open all the time during my grandfather's lifetime. It is also known by its other name S'lat Rabbi Semahya, which was, according to residents of the quarter, the largest synagogue of the *mellah* Al Bali, and today serves as a mosque for the Friday prayer. At present, the mosque remains the only place of Muslim prayer in the old *mellah*. An imam conducts the daily prayer in the mosque, while a *khatib*, assigned by the Ministry of Endowments and Religious Affairs, conducts the Friday prayer service.

The Transition

Residents cite the years of either 1965 or 1968 as the times of the foundation of the mosque. An addendum on the obverse of the bill of sale details the transfer of the *masjid* and of the commercial establishments on the ground floor to a *waqf* ([Islamic] religious endowment) on 17 November 1969, less than a month after the conclusion of the legal sale. All those we asked linked the establishment of the mosque to the transfer of the ground-floor properties to the *waqf* of Moulay Hachem, buyer of the Berdugo house. The mosque can accommodate a hundred worshippers. An imam and a *mouzen* (muezzin) officiated at the dedication; the mosque has no minaret, but four loudspeakers on the top floor of the house broadcast the call to prayer.

The transfer of the site of prayer from Judaism to Islam resulted in other important changes. Two ruined houses next to the synagogue were purchased and annexed in order to enlarge the prayer hall and provide space for a hall of ablutions. This period—the expansion of the space of the synagogue—has been forgotten by residents of the quarter, who assume that the mosque takes up the total space of the synagogue. Thus, they assert that S'lat Berdugo was the largest synagogue of the quarter, though actually the synagogue took up no more than a quarter of the space of the current mosque. Once the construction was done, a *sadaqa* (a ceremony consisting of the hosting of a meal and the recitation of the Koran) was held inside the mosque. Did the *sadaqa* mark the conversion of the site or was it simply a ritual meal marking the opening of the mosque? It is hard to tell. The current imam, who was head of a Quranic school in the old *mellah* at the time, asserted categorically that no conversion ritual was performed: "We simply cleaned and dusted the place, as it had not been in use for quite a while, and we arranged the room in order to lay down the prayer rugs." Apparently, the imam was unaware of the major renovations that took place. He briefly reported that Islam only requires ordinary rules of cleanliness in order to pray at a site belonging to the *People of the Book*.

Conversion

Thus, we find a variety of discourses concerning the conditions of the transformation of the synagogue into a mosque. Some declare that a particular ritual needed to be performed; they use the term *tahroura*, which refers to the "circumcision" of the synagogue. Thus, a local shoemaker said, "It was a *jamaa* (place of prayer) of the Jews which became a jama'a of the Muslims [...] It's like when you marry a Jewess and you convert her to Islam."

For the imam of the mosque, this transformation was a completely valid act within Islam. He based his judgment on the Jews' and Muslims' shared belief in the same divinity: "We can pray in a place where Jews pray. It is not a problem. We are the same, the Jews and us. They love God and we do the same thing. The difference is in the messengers."

Thus, for the imam, according to Islamic law Muslims have the right to appropriate a Jewish place of prayer if Jews have left it, but the opposite may not be done: "We have the right of succession (to inherit their places of prayer), whereas they do not have the right. A Jew may not be heir to a Muslim."

The theologians we spoke to agree that the confessional identity of places of prayer in Islam is unimportant. In their point of view, it is legal to pray in a place of prayer of Judaism, Christianity, Hinduism, and the like. What counts is that the place that comes in contact with the body of the worshipper should not be dirtied by ritually impure substances such as blood, alcohol, urine, etc. Apparently, not all the informants knew the exact steps of the transformation of the synagogue into mosque, whereas the memory of the existence of the Jewish place of prayer does form part of the collective memory of the quarter. It does not evoke any particular attitude or negative reaction, as exists in the case of other synagogues transformed into mosques, for example in Oran (Khiat 2010).

Transformation of a Place of Prayer: Migration and the Re-Appropriation of Space

The point of view most widely accepted in the quarter today emphasizes the departure of the Jews and the absence of a place of prayer for the Muslims. The inhabitants know that the mosque was opened in a place that served as a synagogue. The ground floor's transfer to the *waqf* by the buyer of the Berdugo house is also known. The informers estimate that from 1965 to 1968, the years mentioned as the foundation time of the mosque of Slaouats Street, there were no more than a dozen Jews left in the quarter, most of them artisans (*snayyiya-s*) and small tradesmen of the same socio-economic class as their Muslim neighbours. The synagogue was closed for several years preceding the opening of the mosque. "The Jews (of the old *mellah*) prayed in the new *mellah* or in a *jamaa* opposite the fountain (in the old *mellah*)," said a veteran of the quarter. At that time, there was no place of prayer for Muslims in the old *mellah*.

According to some informers, the transformation of the mosque into a synagogue was the result of the collective action of the Muslim residents, now the majority, to acquire a mosque. Given the absence of a place of Muslim prayer in the quarter, the inhabitants formed a committee to present the problem to the religious authorities of the town (the delegation of the Ministry of Endowments and Religious Affairs). Given the lack of an empty plot of land on which they could erect a mosque, the representatives of the ministry asked the residents to find a place that could serve as a place of prayer. Representatives of the neighbourhood, led by a local delegate who lived opposite the Berdugo house, founded the S'lat Berdugo. Thus, in coordination with the owner, they proposed the purchase of the two ruined houses to annex them to the former synagogue and transform the entire property into a mosque.

Differing Memories of the Jewish Quarter

This episode offers an interesting standpoint for analyzing the transformation of Jewish quarters in Morocco in the period after independence. Thus, we witness two types of re-appropriation of space in those quarters: On the one hand, there is a shared memory of conviviality that we still can see through the architecture of the *mellahs* (old and new); on the other hand, the suppression of Jewish street names bears witness to erasing that presence altogether.

A Shared Memory

The Jewish past of the two quarters (the old and the new *mellahs*) continues to speak through the architecture of the buildings: the shape of the balconies in the new *mellah*, which were built only by certain masons who lived during the period of Jewish presence; the Stars of David, which may be seen here and there on the facades; the interior passages between one house and another—particular to the old *mellah*—as well as communal and religious institutions (synagogues, schools, dispensaries, etc.); the imposing cemetery of the old *mellah*, with its tombs abutting the walls of Moulay Ismail, the new cemetery. This past is still present in memories, mainly nostalgic, of the generations who lived during the Jewish period, as well as in the stories told by younger people to whom the stories were transmitted by their families. The informants mention vague memories of Jewish holidays, as well as Jewish sites such as the school, the synagogues (S'lat Laazimi, S'lat Boussidan, S'lat Berdugo) and other communal institutions.

The Suppression of Traces of Jewish Life

In the late 1970s, the old *mellah* underwent a project of conversion of its streets (*derbs*). Three streets with Jewish religious significance were given Islamic names. Thus, Slaouats Street, where the Berdugo house was located, which referred to the place of prayer of the Jews of the quarter, was baptized Al-Ghufranei, forgiveness, as if to signify the divine deliverance from the "error" represented by the Jewish religion. According to Ahmed, it was his father, the buyer of the Berdugo house, who initiated the change of the street name.

Hakham Street (Saints Street) now bears the name of an imam, Imam Al-Boussari, a religious official and poet who lived in Egypt in the thirteenth century. *Derb Laazimi* (Laazimi Street), which adjoined the synagogue of the same name, S'lat Laazimi, is now Ibn Hani Street, named after an Andalusian poet of the tenth century. Only names with no religious significance remain unchanged: *derb Al-Ghandour, derb al Kayiss* (allegedly a Jewish figure of the *mellah*), *derb Lamtamar* (lit.: "granary"), *derb el-kharrazines* (the shoemakers' street). The changing of the names of streets of the old *mellah* was gradual. It resulted from the complaints of several residents and Muslim notables who saw their residence on streets with Jewish names as an insult to their standing as good Muslims.

Politics and Religion: The Erasure of Jewish Spaces

The most surprising change would take place later, at the time of the changing of the names of the *mellahs* in the early 1980s. The name of the quarter itself was changed from Mellah al Bali (old *mellah*) to Al-Fath. This was hardly an unintentional change. *Al-Fath* in Arabic derives from the root *fth*, signifying opening, conquering, winning, placing on the right path, etc. In the Muslim lexicography, *fath* signifies Muslim conquests and the Islamization of the conquered. Thus, the conquest is emptied of its violent and war-related significance. The Islamization of the conquered peoples becomes an act of divine benevolence, which enables the errant to regain the *Way of Salvation*. Thus, the choice of the name Al-Fath for the old *mellah* follows the same logic of "de-judaization" and Islamization that we witnessed in the renaming of the streets of the *mellah*. Thus, the Mellah Al-Bali becomes the object of an action of *fath*, a new religious marking of its space.

The initiator of the *fath* (conquest) of the old *mellah* was the socialist municipal council, which ruled the city from 1983 to 1992. Only the name of the quarter was changed by the council, whereas the street names were spared. It was in the new *mellah* that a widespread project of de-judaization took place, among all the streets of the quarter. The new *mellah* was renamed Hay Riyad, the name of the place prior to its birth as a Jewish quarter in the 1920s. All the street names of the new *mellah* were changed, except for Palestine Avenue (the commercial and leisure centre in the quarter previously, the Boulevard of the Jews, as it was called) and Market Street. According to one municipal official, the archives recording this action are lost. We find new names such as Deir Yassin (that refers to the massacre of Deir Yassin, near Jerusalem, in 1948), Al-Ourdun (Jordan), Sinai, Al-Aqaba, Hottayne (referring to the battle of Karnei Hittin, between Saladin and the Christian armies in 1187, which brought on the end of the Crusader Kingdom of Jerusalem), Al-Khalil (Hebron), Mahmoud Hamchari (former representative of the PLO in France, assassinated in 1973), Hassan Al Ansari (one of the companions of the Prophet), Ammar ben Yasser (another companion of the Prophet), and Shahid ("martyr") Abderrahmane Amazghar (a Moroccan member of the Arab Liberation Front, killed during a military operation in the north of Israel in 1975).

Petahia Berdugo Street (or Raphael Berdugo, according to another informant) was renamed Salah Eddine El Ayoubi-Saladin. Ibn Maimoune (Maimonides) Street was renamed after an unknown figure, according to an informant, by the name of Abdelsalem Mezgueldi. Israelite Cemetery Street, which borders the new cemetery, became Ibn Zidoun Street, named after an Andalusian poet of the eleventh century. David Street became Ammar ben Yasser, Al-Madrasi Al-Israila Street (Jewish Schools Street) became Maarif (lit.: "knowledge"). The name Jerusalem Street became Al-Quds.

The new names manifest a logic other than that which guided the renaming of certain streets of the old *mellah*. In the old *mellah*, only the street names with Jewish religious significance were gradually modified, in response to the requests of notables and residents of the quarter, who wanted to guard their reputations as good Muslims. In the new *mellah*, it was an action initiated by the municipal council, in which all the names were changed at once. While the new names reflect a wide variety of registers (religious, political, historical, and artistic), the majority refers to the Israeli-Palestinian conflict. By referring directly to the conflict, a new modality was introduced into the relation with Moroccan Judaism.

This renaming of sites is currently the focus of mobilization in both *mellahs*, especially among the younger generation. In the old *mellah*, the repeated visits of descendants of Jewish families alerted the population as to the value of their site. Signs with the new name of the old *mellah*, Hay Al-Fath, have been removed. The younger generation reclaims the Jewish past of the quarter. The *shmisha* (little sun), which decorates the old fountain at the centre of the old *mellah* has become the symbol of that past. Some denounce the de-judaization of the quarter, calling it a racist, criminal, catastrophic, or idiotic act. "Why only the Jewish names and not all the others?," one young tradesman of the old *mellah* asked. These people believe that Jewish heritage is a means of development of their residential space. They are strongly opposed to the local authorities and the Medina Association, which specializes in the protection of the heritage of the old city, judging their actions to be selective and partial.

Conclusion

As a result of this research, my grandfather now appears in a different light than his brothers who moved to the Ville Nouvelle in the 1930s. The affirmation of a Judeo-Arab identity, including a language of its own (Judeo-Arabic), a self-definition that ignored French colonization, social practices determined by daily Jewish-Muslim relations—these were the determinant aspects of his life, even if they are absent from Jewish and Arab collective memory. The history of his house reflects the divergent paths of re-appropriation of space. The built heritage still bears traces of Jewish presence, but Judeo-Arabic is no longer spoken or written, and this modest synagogue has been transformed into a mosque in a quarter that had none. The streets have been renamed in order to erase all Jewish presence in the old and new *mellahs*. Notwithstanding the reconstruction of some synagogues, mainly by the Museum of Moroccan Judaism in Casablanca, most Jewish sites of prayer have undergone an unenviable evolution (Miller 2011). In Meknès, we witness two ways of renaming the sites: political and/or religious. This case raises the issue of the memory of the Jewish population and the heritagization of its traces in the urban space.

More globally, the problematic nature of the memory of Moroccan Judaism may be witnessed in the conflict between politics and religion, a conflict that the past intimacies of living together cannot diminish. The traditional religious register that—by attributing the status of *Dhimma* to Jews—inspired my grandfather's confidence, no longer exists. In the modern political register, this shared memory is denied or effaced by the Israeli-Palestinian conflict. The passage from a traditional religious register (which regulated the relations between a Jewish minority and a Muslim majority, as expressed through the Islamization of some of the street names of the old *mellah*) to a modern political register (the Israeli-Palestinian conflict) explains the new names given to the sites of the new *mellah*.

If in 2011 the new constitution lists the recognition of Judaism as an integral part of Moroccan identity, we wonder if it means a desire to insert Morocco in contemporary modernity, distancing it from ideological control of politics. By erasing the Jewish presence and then by having "second thoughts" about the process of erasure, we can see this process as an attempt to maintain a balance between religious pluralism—which, more than ever before, is the mark of contemporary democratic diversity—and religious hegemony.

CHAPTER 2

Zionism, Colonialism, and Post-Colonial Migrations: Moroccan Jews' Memories of Displacement

Yolande Cohen

The conditions that led a million Jews to leave their Muslim lands to construct new lives elsewhere, mainly in Israel, raise many questions regarding their migrations (Cohen 2019). For the several hundred thousand who left the colonial and national spaces of North Africa for Israel, for cities in metropolitan France, and somewhat later for Canada, especially Montreal, Quebec, the question of their mass migration in a relatively short period of time gives rise to divergent interpretations. The emigration of Jews from Morocco to Israel, in particular, is the subject of intense debate among historians. For some, it signals a real displacement of populations achieved by Israeli Zionist organizations in need of a labour force to populate the new State (Chétrit 2004). For others, it is an exodus, encouraged by the international Zionist organizations, which was rooted in the desire of these Jews to escape the humiliations and abuses committed against them in the name of the *Dhimma* (Bin-Nun 2004).[1] And for the few hundred

---

[1] *Dhimma* is a set of Islamic laws regulating the relationship of Muslims and non-Muslims in a Muslim state. Enforcing the rules of *Dhimma* varied over history, and the traditional way of viewing Jews as subordinate to the Muslims, while recognizing

Jews still living in Morocco, it is an ongoing history of displacement that leaves them with a heritage to preserve for the Jewish diaspora. Such diverging views of those events signal the difficulty of telling a unified story of this moment. I want to contribute to this debate by showing that the combining and often opposing forces of colonialism and Zionism were the main factors that triggered these migrations, in a period of rising Moroccan nationalism. But those forces were also seen as opportunities by some migrants to seize the moment to better their fate and realize their dreams. If we cannot assess every migrant story, I want here to suggest, through my family's experience and memory and other collected oral histories, how we could intertwine those memories to a larger narrative to shed more light on this history.[2] I also want to illustrate how the push and pull forces that led to Moroccan Jewry's migrations between the 1940s and 1960s were the result of a reordering of the complex relationships between the different ethnic and religious communities well before the migration took place.

Colonialism and Zionism: A Brief Overview

Since its installation in Morocco in 1863, the Alliance israélite universelle grew rapidly all over the country, as an extension of French colonialism, which wanted to teach French and Western Culture to Jewish populations in the Mediterranean. As an agent of the colonial power, but also as a way to revitalize Jewish diaspora, Alliance had built a network of schools, which gave the colonial administration its workforce, for both its administrative and military needs. Its main purpose was to keep Jews in Morocco as emissaries or middlemen between the French colonial power and the Moroccan *Maghzen* or government. Neither the Alliance nor the French government expected the Moroccan

---

and respecting their places of worship and religion, has been a pervading feature of this relationship through the contemporary era.

[2] This chapter presents the results of a larger research project on the migrations of Moroccan Jews in France and Canada, funded by a Social Sciences Research Council of Canada grant (2014–2019). For the use of oral history narratives in this research, see also Cohen, Messika, and Cohen Fournier, 2015. For the purposes of this chapter, I relied on unpublished oral interviews and written correspondence with Moshe Cohen, son of Itshak Cohen. He sent me the original material he found at the Zionist Archives in Israel on his father as well as some family archives.

Jews to become French, a citizenship they granted only to Algerian Jews with the famous Crémieux Decree of 1870, therefore discouraging their migration to France. The many thousands Jews who sent their children to Alliance schools to learn French soon discovered that they were in a dire situation, uprooted from their traditions and languages, but not fully accepted as part of the French community. Westernized, they nevertheless kept their traditions and most of their community organizations and rituals.

A competing force, Zionism, was also present in Morocco. Its religious and mystical version, which held a millenarian view of return to Zion, was impregnating the traditional religious population and was found everywhere in some form or other. It was present in some cities, like Meknès: my paternal grandparents were ardent Zionists, although nothing appears in the family history about being convinced by anyone about Zionism or being linked to any Zionist organization. Their belief was that someday they would be able to realize their dream to live in Eretz Israël (the Land of Israel). Itshak Cohen tried to move to Palestine when he got married, as witnessed by a letter answering Itshak's quest for immigration papers for the enlarged family dated 1935. Many other orthodox and less orthodox Jews shared the religious ideal of moving to Zion. But it is mostly the contemporary secular and political Zionism that drew them to Israel after 1948, sometimes systematically emptying whole villages of their Jews, especially in the Atlas Mountains, for instance, but not only there; almost 80 percent of the Jewish population went to Israel with the help of Zionist organizations (Trigano 2009).

There are many differences between the various waves of Aliyah, which led almost 120,000 Jews from Morocco to Israel in less than 10 years following the creation of the state. The extent of this migration in such a short period of time could certainly lead us to consider that Zionism was the Jews' answer to colonialism; in other words, Zionism won over French colonialism as a pull factor, if we just consider those numbers and the fact that it happened between 1948 and 1956. It is another question to know whether those people went to Israel voluntarily, or because France failed them, or they had no other choice, etc.

It is admittedly a difficult question to answer, since no one knows exactly how those decisions are taken and how the policies that were decided for them affected them. One thing that recent studies stress is the fact that even the migrants to Israel did not lack agency. The fractious colonial society offered them many ways to negotiate their fate and actually gave them some agency in their decision to leave. Depending on their place in the different sectors of the colonial society, one could predict where they migrated (Yaron Tsur 1997, 2001, 2007). The very few who were integrated into the Western sector, went to France. Those in the native sector, composed of Jews deeply entrenched in the local Arab and Berber cultures (and who spoke mainly Arabic or Judeo-Arabic), were either pulled by Zionists or wished to go to Israel. Those who adopted only part of the Occidental culture, while retaining a strong attachment to their Jewishness, went either to Europe, Canada, or South America, depending on their language, their family, or diasporic network. Of course, such a categorization is broad, and one should also include gender, social class, profession, religion, and generational positions to indicate with better accuracy where they migrated and when. This information will only give us an approximation of the path of migrations, since once they left their country of origin, they tended to circulate many times between different poles and axes of the diaspora (France, Israel, Canada for the francophones; Central and Latin America for the Spanish-speaking). My family's migrations are a case in point to illustrate these different patterns.

My Family's Migration Patterns

Raphael Cohen's genealogies had been instrumental in tracing many Moroccan-Jewish ancestors back to ancient times, especially for Meknès' well-known families (Georgette and Raphael Cohen Family database). He was very kind to trace my own genealogy, in which we can track my father's parents (Abraham Cohen and Jamila Ohana) and my mother's parents (Eliezer Berdugo and Simha Toledano). All four of my grandparents were born in the 1880s and died at a relatively young age, in the 1940s in Meknès (but my maternal grandmother, Simha Toledano [Berdugo], died in 1972, prompting my mother to postpone her own family's departure till 1974). On the Berdugo side of my mother's family, all five of her uncles were born and died in Meknès, but an aunt went to Israel and died there. My grandmother Simha Toledano had only two siblings, who were born and died in Meknès. But of my mother's six siblings, all were born in Meknès between 1910 and 1935, none are buried in Meknès: Two died in France, three in Montreal, and two are still alive, one in Montreal and one in Paris. Westernized in the Alliance schools, even though the father insisted on living in the old Jewish quarter or *mellah* of Meknès until his death, this family is an archetype of migration within the colonial landscape. In one generation, between my grandparents and my parents, everyone moved to a francophone society (France or Quebec). Before that move, Raphael Cohen has been able to date back to eleven generations of Berdugos that resided in Meknès.

We cannot trace with such certainty my Cohen family ancestry. But for my father's family, whose belief in religious Zionism was absolute, the only place to go was Israel. Very early on, my grandfather Abraham Cohen was eager to get British or French protection and passport (letter dated 30 December 1918 from the French resident Lyautey to Abraham Cohen). He wrote letters to almost every official that could grant him and his family a passage to Israel, then Palestine, under the British mandate. Unfortunately, he did not succeed: He and his wife died before they could see the creation of the State of Israel. Their dream would be realized by their children, who took their remains from their graves in Meknès to Jerusalem, where they are now buried. Of their ten children, born in Meknès between 1910 and 1930, half of them went to Israel. My aunts and uncles quickly settled in with their large families and became Israeli citizens, except for two uncles who decided to leave Israel in 1955 and came back to Casablanca, Morocco, where they became successful businessmen (only to move again to France in the 1970s).

Leaving for Israel: Zionism and Fragmented Memory

When and how did my family members feel that they were no longer at home in their own country? This perception happened for most of them long before their actual departure. We were able to interview three members of the Cohen family, Aaron and his two youngest sisters Anna and Marguerite, who confirmed that the family atmosphere was already filled with the Zionist ideal of going to Eretz Israel. Since the 1920s, their father, Abraham Cohen, a very religious and observant Jew, had been trying to convince the British Consulate to give his large family visas to enter Palestine. They have not only the memory of those discussions, but David Cohen has a copy of the letter that he wrote in 1923 to the British Consulate to that effect. When their father died, his dream became the family's dream. As we saw, it was Itshak's (his eldest son) fate to carry it on, as he managed to depart with his own family of seven, his brothers and their families, and his two younger sisters in 1948. My father, Aaron, the youngest of the boys, who had just married my mother in 1948, left Meknès also to join them in Israel, but they stayed longer in a refugee/transit camp near Marseille. It is unclear why they did not make the move to join all his brothers and sisters who were waiting for him in Israel. He told us that he received news that the situation was not that great for his siblings, who lost all their fortunes and hopes during the 1948 War of Independence and that he should postpone his departure. He stayed longer as an instructor (*Shaliach*) in the transit camp run by the Jewish Agency and Hebrew Immigrant Aid Society (HIAS) in Aubagne and then had to leave the camp, since he was not departing. With his wife and daughter (me), they finally went back to Meknès a few years later, settled there and departed for Montreal later, in 1974. They followed his wife's sister's family who had settled there in the late 1960s. While he remained in Morocco, it meant that he could not see his own brothers and sisters in Israel for almost 30 years.

The actualization of the family's Zionist ideal justified the breaking up with their own siblings, family, and land. In this context, the rupture with their immediate environment was brutal: Everyone in the family had to keep the secret of a clandestine departure. This event became a secret, which would haunt them later. For my father's two younger sisters, Anna and Marguerite, who were brought to Israel like "a package in their brother's luggage," by flight to Marseille and by ship to Haifa where they settled while only 13 and 15 years old, this story is anything but a nice memory! They still resent their sudden departure from their home, leaving their bicycles on the street, with little or nothing at all, and their harsh transplantation to a country totally unknown to them. Their memory of Morocco is, therefore, totally enshrined in a veil of fear, the only thing now that could have justified their sudden exile.

Zionism was the main motivation for their departure to Israel. The Zionist ideal of their parents was of a religious type: For them, it was the return to Zion. Whereas for their children, especially their two older boys, it was both the religious aspect and the ideal to build their own country that prompted them to leave as soon as the State of Israel was created. They were proud to say that no one helped them to migrate, that it was their money and desire that brought them to Eretz Israel, not so for the tens of thousands of people who left during the three major waves of Aliya between 1948 and 1956. The clandestine work of the Zionist organizations was not acknowledged openly, but the rumours of the help they provided to people who wanted to leave was known. In villages in the south and in the Atlas Mountains, where those communities have been living for many generations, the Zionist organizations were instrumental in organizing their collective departure to Israel, in buses and boats. Whole villages fled, leaving behind their homes, schools, places of worship, cemeteries, and a vibrant Jewish life.

A case in point is the unknown story of my uncle Itshak Cohen who created an immigrant association in 1949 (Irgoun Ole-Zfon Africa) to defend and represent North African Jews, whom he considered discriminated against by the Israeli establishment. The clash between his Zionist ideal and the reality he discovered there could not have been more acute. Well before the Black Panthers movement fought for them, denouncing their plight as Black Jews or Arab Jews, he demanded respect for his group of migrants, who left everything they had to join in the creation of a Jewish state. His was a strong ideal, inherited from his parents as a religious calling, but also to build a country of their own. Contrary to European Zionism, with its millenarian accents, his was a strong belief in one people, one state. So, his disappointment was complete and long-lasting, when he saw that no one cared about those migrants in Israel. One of several letters that he wrote to different Israeli institutions to warn them about the harm that North African Jews were enduring, outlined some of his grievances (letters in Hebrew from Itshak Cohen, *Comité de la communauté Israélite d'Afrique du Nord*, 24 July 1949, and in French, to Mr. Chetrit, Israel Police minister, 7 December 1949), to no avail. He lost his fortune and ended up very bitter, impacting his entire family of nine children, dispersed all over the world, while Moshe tells us his story with amazement in his voice.[3]

My family's migration patterns were determined both by the big events of a period marked by the Shoah, the end of World War II, and

---

[3] "My father is a 'notable': he was associated with his father in importing goods from Great-Britain for all of Morocco; they made lots of money [...] My father had a large family of nine (Yaffa deceased), who are now all over the world: Moshe (lawyer in Haifa), Marie (New York), Shmuel (Geneva and now in Israel), Daniel (captain in the Commercial Marine, who died recently), Gabriel (Zurich), Shlomo (Côte d'Ivoire and Israel), Shochana (in Israel). He was educated with Rav Messas, one of the brightest students in their Yeshiva, speaking and writing French perfectly" (Interview with Moshe Cohen, August 2018 and May 2019).

the decolonization process, of which Zionism and colonialism were by-products, as well as the personal agency of their members. The period of 1940s was the decisive moment in which their fate was sealed: Whether they went to France or Israel, in the first or second or third wave of migrations, they knew that they could not stay in Morocco any longer as a vibrant Jewish community. In this story, there is no one thing that emerges as a cause of departure, but a web of small events, unrelated to each other, which stem from the memories of people we have interviewed.

Fractured Memories of Departures

Individual trajectories only illustrate some trends, but in the absence of a unified story, I used oral history interviews to document Moroccan Jews' memories of their departures (Cohen and Messika 2012; Cohen Fournier and Messika 2015). This study draws on interviews collected in Montreal and in Paris, with sixty-four individuals who are native of Morocco. In the sample collected in France, there were natives of Morocco and of Tunisia. In this respect, the first wave of migration, mostly to Israel in 1948, is different from those that took place at the end of the 1950s, after the independence of Morocco.

As we will see, the meta-narrative outlined earlier frames some of the memories transmitted to us by our interviewees, which became pieces in a larger strategy to present their migration as a simple way to better their lives. How are the competing forces of colonialism and Zionism playing in their decisions to migrate? The more neutral term of *migration* will be used to characterize their departure from Morocco, as we let them explain how they saw it, then and now. Far from offering a unified story, the memories collected here show a tapestry of mixed feelings, of decisions taken in haste, and a lack of clear perspective by a group of people who were taken up in the maelstrom of big events and who tried to make the best of them. For the older generation of interviewees, the interviews were conducted at two different moments in time. The first ones were done with older migrants that arrived in Montreal in the 1970s and collected in the 1980s. The second group had been recently interviewed within the Montreal Life Story Project.

Defining the Collectivity

How did the interviewees define the group to which they belong? We find a complex geography of relations between the different groups within colonial society that are altered by independence. The relationships between the French, the Arabs, and the Jews during the colonization of Morocco left lasting traces in their memories. First conviviality, friendship between Jews and Arabs, is mentioned, in particular within work relations for men. Women often kept away from too much public exposure in mixed settings, fearing that their daughters would get forced to marry Muslims (marriages with Catholics being more tolerated). The protection of Jews by the king of Morocco under the Vichy regime is a trope that served to explain their gratitude toward Morocco and to the king. Little is said about their situation as Jews in Morocco or about antisemitism. By contrast, the antisemitism of the French is often emphasized, not only in Morocco but also in France (Abitbol 2010).

Class also played a role in their relations, not only with the other groups (French and Arab) but also within the Jewish community. Léon (born in 1942 in Casablanca) evokes the bad memories that his father kept of Morocco, notably of being relegated, because of his poverty, to the back of the synagogue by the wealthier Jews. His father also had, according to Léon, the memory of having been mistreated by the Arabs and was rather happy because of the French presence. A comparison is also often made with the other Jews of Europe during the Second World War, leading the interviewees to minimize what happened to them as benign events, like stones being thrown and raids in the *mellah*. Admittedly, the memory of the abuses suffered, whether small daily humiliations or some major public events, are relegated to a hazy memory, but are evoked spontaneously by the interviewees (Elbaz 2001; Gottreich and Schroeter 2011; Trigano 2009).

However, these uneven relationships changed with the independence of Morocco in 1956: As the French had no more direct authority over inter-community relations and Moroccan nationalism had won, uncertainty reigned (Rivet 2002). Rumours replaced news, which reinforced their desire to leave: In 1957, it was said that the Jews would be enrolled in the Moroccan army and Léon did not see himself serving and was scared of being drafted to combat against Israel. The awareness of international tensions stemming from the Arab-Israeli conflict revealed potential conflicts between neighbours. The Middle Eastern conflict, which spanned several decades, thus played an important part in the shifting of social relations between the Jewish and Arab communities in Morocco. After independence, Léon mentions that the Arabs suspected the Jews of sustaining—and even of financing—Israel, which created certain tensions (surveillance, ransoms) and a "heavy atmosphere." The clashes between groups in an already segmented society made it difficult to retain their traditional way of life. Everything seemed to be shattered by those big events, while some felt that there was little they could do to change their circumstances. The belief in *Mekhtub* (destiny) will take different forms and shapes in their memory of those events.

Clandestinity

For six interviewees, their departures took place clandestinely. Each of them remembers some element of the story. Freha (born in Casablanca in 1940) recalls that her father had sold half of his property before leaving, but that he could not get his money safely out of the country. He asked his friend, a French colonel, to do the transaction on his behalf, with all the risks related to that. Freha herself, when she departed the second time, was hiding her money in her baby's diapers! Henri (born in Meknès in 1926) remembers his mock departure "we left the house in order, as if we were leaving for the holidays!" Crossing the border into Spain, his car packed with all kinds of things, he feared crossing and being caught at the border. Hiding from their neighbours that they were leaving for good was not easy, as it implied not sharing essential aspects of their lives. In many cases, they went to great lengths in order to hide it carefully. Whom were they hiding from? Were they equally frightened by the local authorities as their Muslim neighbours were? Were they suspicious of their neighbours, who might report them? They obviously were afraid, even in the 1970s when the administration was giving out passports more easily (with some corruption, *bakchich*, or intervention from well-placed friends or business relations). None of them really talked about it. There is a sense of urgency in the packing of their things and in their departure. Even if their decision to leave took a long time to mature, as they say that they had been thinking about it for quite a while, the actual departure happened when there was an opportunity or when they thought that the situation was deteriorating.

There is a striking difference between the individuals in the first wave who had to depart precipitously to an imposed destination, mostly to Israel in 1948, and those who participated in the second waves of migrations, which took place in the 1950s. In their discourses, their departure is the result of an individual or family decision. Their memory of their parents' continuous administrative hassle to seek the notorious papers (visas, administrative authorizations, and sometimes passports) to depart is quite vivid. Jacques (born in Casablanca in 1937) evokes, therefore, his departure for Canada in January 1957, with his father and brother, who obtained their visas from the British Consulate in Casablanca, after seeing a job ad in the newspaper. His mother and sisters, who stayed behind to liquidate their assets, joined them later. Leaving the women behind could be interpreted as a way to signal to the others (the administration, the neighbours, the friends) that it was not a definite departure, but only a (temporary) job-motivated migration. For her part, Freha said that she first left Morocco to join her husband, who was studying medicine in Paris in 1961. Her parents, who went also to France with two of her sisters, finally migrated to Montreal in 1964. She came back two years later, as her husband decided to do his internship in a Moroccan hospital in Casablanca (where his parents lived) only to move back again to Paris, at the birth of her first son. From there they moved to Canada in the 1970s and then to Arizona in the United States where she and her husband settled with their family of four. Finally, when she divorced her husband, Freha left the United States to join the rest of her siblings who were established in Montreal.

Multiple Migrations: Post-Colonial Circulations

It is striking to see the succession of departures and returns, alone, with, or without family, during this period of post-independence of Morocco. Many other interviewees explain these migrations as family-bound, or simply to study or work, as if it were a natural move; even though we know how challenging such migrations were, involving a massive cost in money, time, relations, networks to seek entry, exit permissions, immigration papers, etc. It seems as if there were no other causes for their departure or at least they were erased from their memory. They also insist that they had a choice of destination and going back and forth to Morocco freely is a testament of their ability to decide whether or not to leave. Canada was the foremost choice, for it is far away from colonial France and newly independent Morocco. In the midst of the fierce political battles that were conducted by international Jewish organizations like Jewish Immigrant Aid Services (JIAS) to "save the Jewish community of Morocco," our interviewees have erased such rhetoric from their memories and retained only that they themselves could take this opportunity to leave (Messika 2015). Our interviewees' itineraries were complex, as they moved from one place to another within a diasporic triangle: Israel, France, Canada, and/or when possible, the United States. They stopped for some time in one country and returned to Casablanca, and finally left Morocco completely. Their families were dispersed along the road in different destinations and eventually gathered in one place. Léon's parents left Morocco for Israel in 1946 (after six months spent in a camp in Marseille), came back to France in the 1950s, and left again for Israel in 1965 with their younger children, only to come back to France in the 1960s, and then move to Montreal in the 1970s. Their migrations resemble a patchwork of the eternal migrant or "wandering Jew." Once they left their country of origin, they did not find a place to stay long enough to call it their home!

In these interviews, one gets a sense of loss, but it is not explicit. They are in a survival mode, so the relationships with others are secondary, not important, not worth recalling. They do not even tell us if they discussed the decisions to leave within their own family. The overall impression is one of a quick departure, with no one really in charge of taking care of such details as the destination of the family migration and the explanation of the cause of their departure. In Henri's family, the oldest son decided to bring his two younger sisters to Israel with him, after their parents died and just when the State of Israel was founded, in the summer of 1948. He even rented a house in Marseille for all of them to wait for their papers. In Léon's family, as the oldest son of a family of nine, he worried about the education of his younger brothers and helped them emigrate to Canada. Around him, the family will finally reunite in Montreal. His preoccupation is inward, within the family unit, not with the outside world, which is perceived as malevolent, scary, and not to be trusted.

In many interviews, the same feeling of powerlessness of those hard times pervades the interviewees' memory. Even if they identify *a posteriori* one factor that triggered their own departure and their families, there is also a general atmosphere in the community that played a major role in their decision to leave. One of them told us "Everybody was leaving, so we had to leave as well." Their segregation from the rest of the Moroccan people in the *mellah* and their subtle exclusion from the Western world, even when some of them moved away to live in the Westernized city (Ville Nouvelle), brought on a strong feeling of alienation. They indeed did some business with the other communities, some even went to the same French schools, but the strict separation between those different sectors was quite effective in keeping them from mingling with each other. They quickly learned to keep their stories to themselves and not share the more intimate details about their lives with anyone else. Even within the Jewish community, the sharing of information was not open, and rumours replaced facts.

Leaving for the Children

These events are but a backstory behind the factor, often cited as determining their departure: Parents saw little future for their children in Morocco. Even if their economic situation is considered by Henri to be flourishing, the decision to leave "for the children" takes over. Some children, for that matter, left for Paris to study (the older girl in Henri's family or Freha's husband) before their parents' departure. We can also notice that within families, there is a concern for the education of girls (who can leave home and change countries for this reason). As the issue of the children's education is often cited as one of the reasons justifying the family's departure, focusing on this aspect of student migration allows us to establish the influence of French-Jewish colonialism.

The narratives highlight the importance of Alliance israélite universelle schools. In 1956, the institution enrolled nearly 33,000 students in Morocco and held a major role in the transmission of Jewish and French education, even if some of the children could attend French schools and all these French and Alliance schools were competing with the religious education offered by Talmud Torah schools (Kaspi 2010; Laskier 1994). Even though the Alliance israélite universelle was a Jewish institution, it was a vector of Westernization and there were tensions with traditionalist families who wanted mostly a Jewish education. The distinction between the education received in the French schools and the education received in the schools of the Alliance israélite universelle is not as clear-cut. There were several transfers from one school to the other and it was common to receive part of one's education in a school of the Alliance and then in a French lycée. The high quality and the prestige of the French lycées seemed to have drawn the parents to enroll their children.

The way in which these stories play down the existing tension between Jewish and secular education gives an indication of the attractiveness of French culture; it gave them the possibility to navigate within several school systems. The centrality of French culture constitutes a crucial experience in Morocco, where the French presence was the most recent in North Africa and where the colonial society was still organized around established communities. Certain narratives concerning French culture reflect the idea of a possible emancipation and of a possible rupture with the traditional world. This may take a gendered dimension. Indeed, the women emphasize their mother's or grandmother's will for them to pursue their education. It also gives us insights into the family and gender dynamics that were expressed during the confrontation with the French educational institutions. For the men we interviewed, attending school was not accompanied by the same militancy.

The Ethnicization of Social Relations

The majority of these stories seem to follow the existing social and community segmentation of the colonial world. In these narratives, the Arab-Muslim world is absent, and the interviewees focus on evocations of the family or of French culture. Fear is seldom present in the narratives of the people interviewed, who left their countries when they were younger, in contrast to the interviews conducted with older Moroccan Jews, who had a profession and children. Due to the social stratification and the ethnicization of relations within colonial society, the Arab-Muslim society is a seldom-cited motive of migration in our narratives. For many, the previous departure of members of their family to Israel, Paris, or Montreal determined their own. It was as if the whole community was taken by this wave of migration. Their profound disengagement from their own life made me think as if their belonging to the Jewish community (which was an extension of their family, their clan, or their sector) represented their connection to the outside world.

They considered migrating as something quite "natural" for the generation who grew up in the French colonial system. The younger generation (the baby boomers, who grew up when Morocco succeeded in gaining its independence from France) were the principal actors of the decision to migrate. In some cases, they were old enough to decide for themselves and the family followed suit; for others, their future (jobs, alliances, etc.) was the reason their parents gave for moving their family away.

The departures of the people interviewed are inscribed both in collective and family memories, but were organized in secret, away from the gaze of the others, particularly that of non-Jewish neighbours. Belonging to a sector of the colonial world, while still prevalent in their narratives, is blurred by another aspect of post-colonial life in Morocco, that is the cultural/education nexus. Depending on where one has been educated and socialized, the combined effects of colonialism and Zionism strongly impacted the time of their departures and the places they went to.

The creation of the State of Israel was a strong pull factor for those people who, like my father's family, were eager to go to the land of their forefathers. The pull was rapidly reinforced by a push factor, which was exercised by Zionist organizations among local indigenous populations. Its effect was massive, since most of those people did not have much to say and went along according to plans devised for them. Soon after the independence of Morocco, the future of those who considered themselves part of the Westernized sector, like my mother's family, appeared suddenly blocked, even though our interviewees present their migration as a means of improving their lot. They decided to depart, and they think of their migration as a non-coerced choice.

The destinations differ according to the sectors and to the combined action of Zionism and colonialism; the non-occidental majority was pulled very early on to migrate to Israel by the strong Zionist organizations, whereas colonial France accepted very few migrants from Morocco, having at the same time to relocate a million French citizens after the Algerian War. The population of this Westernized sector tried first France and then Canada (or Latin America for the hispanophones). Also noteworthy is the difference in the temporality of these migrations: After the migrations of the mainly French and Christians to their country of citizenship, Jews migrated in the 1950s through the 1970s, whereas their Muslim neighbours migrated later, from 1980 to 2000. It is striking to see how the cognitive and memory processes of those migrants have blocked the trauma associated with their migration. The thing that remains vibrant is their feeling of belonging to a lost world. As Moshe recounts the story of his father, which he carefully documents, digging out letter after letter from the trove of the Zionist archives, he looks back to this world with amazement, wondering how his family has made it through it all.

PART II

Between Paris and Montreal

CHAPTER 3

Marriage and Mobility of Moroccan Jews in Montreal and Paris

Yolande Cohen and Martin Messika

Canada's Jewish population is diverse (Cohen and Messika 2023).[1] One of its main divisions is between Ashkenazim, who were the majority, and Sephardim, who also boast a rich history in Canada. Ashkenazim are said to derive from the Roman exile in 70 CE, Sephardim from the Babylonian exile, 657 years earlier. Where Muslim Andalusia (the Iberian Peninsula) influenced Sephardi culture, Christian Europe influenced Ashkenazi culture.

When Christians completed their reconquest of the Iberian Peninsula in the late fifteenth century, the Inquisition forced Jews who did not convert to Christianity to flee. Expelled Jews resettled in North Africa, the Habsburg Netherlands, the Italian peninsula, the Ottoman Empire, and elsewhere. Some of them eventually made their way to England. Following the British conquest of New France in 1763, a few immigrated to Montreal. Mainly merchants, these immigrants founded

---

[1] This chapter is a revised version of Messika and Cohen (2017). It was translated from the French by Robert Brym with the assistance of Yolande Cohen and forms part of a larger project on post-colonial migrations of Moroccan Jews, supported by the Social Sciences and Humanities Research Council of Canada. The authors thank Robert Brym for his translation, kind assistance, and thorough editing of the text.

Canada's first congregation, Shearith Israel, and the synagogue named after their countries of origin, the Spanish and Portuguese Synagogue, in 1768.

The legacy of the early Sephardic immigration largely dissipated, but a revitalization occurred when Jews from North Africa, mostly Morocco, felt compelled to leave their countries in the context of European decolonization and growing anti-Jewish sentiment following the creation of the State of Israel. Between the late 1950s and the 1980s, about 15,000 French-speaking Moroccan Jews settled in Montreal, with a smaller, mostly Spanish-speaking Moroccan community preferring Toronto.

According to the 2018 Survey of Jews in Canada, about 90 percent of Canada's Sephardim is divided approximately equally between Toronto and Montreal. In Montreal, they form nearly one quarter of the Jewish population. When respondents were asked in 2018 how connected they felt to Jewish life in their city, the difference between Sephardim and Ashkenazim in the proportion who said "not very connected," "not at all connected," and "don't know" reached statistical significance ($p < 0.01$). The immigrant generation did not always see eye to eye with the English-speaking Ashkenazi majority in Montreal, and Table 3.1 suggests that the sense of estrangement persists in at least part of the Sephardic community today. About three in ten Sephardim feel less well connected to the Canadian-Jewish mainstream than Ashkenazim do.

For two reasons, these results should be treated cautiously. First, the self-identified Sephardi subsample in the 2018 Survey of Jews in Canada is small and heterogeneous, including, like previous surveys, people of North African and Middle Eastern origin. Second, the findings should be tempered with the observation that a 2017 focus group of twenty young Montreal Sephardim expressed stronger attachment to Judaism than to the Montreal-Jewish community. More recent interviews with young Sephardim show the same trend, with a minority active in Hasidic or ultra-Orthodox groups in the Montreal metropolitan area.[2]

---

[2] This is Robert Brym's introductory note to our text.

Table 3.1. "How connected are you to Jewish life in your city?" (2018, percentage)

	Sephardim (n = 207)	Ashkenazim (n = 1,947)
Very	34	40
Somewhat	38	41
Not very/not at all/don't know	28	20
Total	100	101

Note: The second column does not equal 100 due to rounding. An additional 20 respondents self-identified as Mizrahim (Easterners). Adding them to the Sephardim does not significantly change the findings.
Source: Brym, Neuman, and Lenton (2019).

Israel was the main destination of Moroccan-Jewish immigrants in the 1950s, while France and Canada were important secondary centres of immigration. The Jews who immigrated to Canada in the 1960s and 1970s first settled mainly in Greater Montreal. Those who immigrated to France settled mainly in the Paris region. In the latter cases, the immigrants were in their great majority educated in the francophone school system of the Alliance israélite universelle and therefore aspired to be part of the middle class in Morocco and in the countries to which they immigrated (Abitbol 2009).

How did the Moroccan-Jewish population adjust to life in Montreal and Paris? Did immigration consolidate the middle class? Or did migration to Montreal or Paris confirm the hope these migrants had of achieving upward occupational mobility? Comparative analysis makes it possible to understand such specificities of Moroccan-Jewish migration in each urban area (Green 2002). The migration took place over several decades, so one can also ask how the occupational profile of the immigrants changed over the years.

For a long time, the historiography of this immigration movement has centred on men, ignoring women's paths. However, Moroccan-Jewish immigrants, who are sometimes not mentioned in general works on Moroccan immigration, included women as well as men. The present analysis allows us to compare the ways in which men and women adjusted to life in the two cities.

Studies conducted in the years following their arrival show that the immigrants quickly became economically independent (Berman, Nahmiash, and Osmer 1970, 5). Based on the 1971 Canadian census, Jean-Claude Lasry and Claude Tapia (1989) emphasize the importance of the category "office workers and sales personnel," which accounted for 40 percent of North African Jews in Montreal, compared with 14 percent of the general population at the national level. Using an index of occupational status, Lasry also analyzed the career paths of Jews from the Maghreb in Montreal. He established that the early stages of arrival in Montreal corresponded to a period of "prestige loss" and downward mobility. This was particularly the case for individuals who were property owners, members of the liberal professions, and small traders in their country of birth. Nevertheless, opportunities for upward occupational mobility existed for those who became blue-collar workers.

Lasry (1980) found that after seven years in Canada, immigrants were employed in an occupation with the same level of occupational prestige as the one they held in their country of birth. This finding is consistent with that of Naomi Moldofsky (1968), who discovered that the percentage of migrants who felt that the job they held was of higher status than the one they had in their country of birth depended on how long they had been in Canada: 15 percent for those who had been in the country for four years, rising to 40 percent for newcomers who had been in the country for nine years or more. In addition, analyses of the 2001 census and the 2011 National Household Survey reveal a Sephardic Montreal population, including but not limited to Moroccans, that is well integrated into the working world and with a significant number of managers and professionals. It has therefore become common to consider this population as having migrated relatively successfully in comparison with non-Jewish immigrant groups who settled in Montreal at about the same time, such as Portuguese, Haitians, and Italians.

Analysis of the French case reveals similarities, even if Moroccan natives are more difficult to identify since studies include them in the larger category of North African Jews from Tunisia, Morocco, and Algeria. Thus, in her pioneering work, Doris Bensimon (1971) emphasized their economic integration into the French system—without minimizing the difficulties they encountered culturally and emotionally. Compared to Haitians who arrived in France in the same period, Moroccan Jews fared better in terms of their socio-economic status (Cohen and Jabouin 2021).

Sources

This chapter provides a fresh perspective on the settlement of Jews from Morocco by focusing on two dimensions indicating their degree of adjustment in the host society: marriage and occupation. It extends previous work on marriages at Montreal's Spanish and Portuguese Synagogue and two Parisian synagogues (rue Copernic and Synagogue des Tournelles), which highlights the high rate of intermarriage between spouses of North African origin in Montreal and Paris (Cohen and Scioldo-Zürcher 2014). Data on the occupations of newcomers upon arrival in Montreal and Paris derive from information collected by the social service agencies from which they received assistance (Messika 2020). Information at the time of marriage (a stage of stabilization in the host country) is based on files and marriage certificates in Parisian and Montreal synagogues.[3] The study covers the period 1961–1975 in Paris and 1969–2014 in Montreal. To provide a basis for comparing occupations in the two cities, we used the Canadian National Occupational Classification (NOC). This categorization was refined by identifying job categories not included in the NOC.

Arrival in Montreal and Paris

The profile of Moroccan-Jewish immigrants and the conditions of their settlement differed from the profile and settlement conditions of other immigrants who arrived in Canada after the Second World War. For example, unlike Italians, they almost all arrived with their families, were more highly skilled occupationally, and settled in urban centres. In Montreal, their settlement was supported by Jewish associations such as Jewish Immigrant Aid Services (JIAS), which offered financial assistance and help finding housing and employment. Analysis of social agency files allows us to compose a socio-professional profile of the newcomers and offer a partial assessment of their social situation and professional background.

In their country of birth, the majority of men had been employed as office workers (including accountants; 29 percent) or craft workers (22 percent). The majority of women (53 percent) had at least one previous paying job. Among those who worked in the paid labour force, 48 percent of Moroccan-born women had been office workers (secretaries or clerks), while 27 percent worked as dressmakers, hairdressers, and the like.

---

[3] We thank Veronique Cahen and Christine Chevalier-Caron, who entered data from the marriage certificates.

This snapshot of the Moroccan-Jewish population upon arrival in Montreal reveals a relatively skilled population, among which office jobs predominated for both men and women. Nevertheless, during their settlement, men and women followed different paths to paid work, reflecting a period of adjustment in their return to employment. For men, arrival in Montreal was often associated with a change in employment sector. Thus, only 49 percent of men who were office workers or accountants in Morocco, and who found their first job in Montreal with the assistance of a social worker, were able to work in their previous field of employment. This phenomenon is common among immigrants, testifying to the difficulties they have initially in finding the same kind of job they had in their country of origin.

Women's labour force participation rates fell substantially after they arrived in Montreal.[4] This finding is consistent with other studies that show that the percentage of North African Jewish women without work in the paid labour force is higher in Montreal than in their country of birth. The difference can be explained by the structure of the Montreal labour market, which can be less welcoming for women than for men. In addition, JIAS social workers may have been more concerned with finding a job for the "male head of household" than for their wives and daughters (Néméh-Nombré 2017).

In the French case, analysis of reception files allows us to sketch a profile of the newcomers. In her analysis of social services offered by the Fonds social juif unifié in Toulouse, Colette Zytnicki highlighted the importance of the employed population, comprising 29 percent of its clients. Workers and service personnel represented 18 percent of the employed clients, craft workers 14 percent, and tradespeople 15.7 percent (Zytnicki 1998, 155). In Paris, at the Comité d'action sociale israélite de Paris, 35 percent of Moroccan-born people worked in occupations close to the craft industry, representing a larger percentage than office workers in Montreal. This difference may be related to source bias but may also be the result of more highly qualified Jewish populations immigrating to Canada, the latter having been selected by Canadian immigration authorities partly for their socio-occupational profile, which was not the case in France.

---

[4] In the sample, only 23 percent of Moroccan-born women (sixty-three people) held a job at least once before their follow-up interview.

Marriage Record Samples

Collection of data for the period 1955–1970 began at Montreal's Spanish and Portuguese Synagogue and in two Parisian synagogues, a consistorial synagogue on rue des Tournelles and a liberal synagogue on rue Copernic. The earlier research is developed here in two ways. First, in addition to marriages celebrated at Montreal's Spanish and Portuguese Synagogue, we include marriages that took place at Montreal's Or Hahayim Synagogue, which has a large Moroccan membership. In addition, complementary research was carried out at the Consistoire de Paris for synagogues in the Paris region, bringing together diverse places of worship, including synagogues established as chapels.

The Montreal sample consists of 1,834 marriages celebrated in the Spanish and Portuguese Synagogue and Or Hahayim. Between these two synagogues, 665 marriages were celebrated between 1969 and 1979, another 629 between 1980 and 1989, 261 between 1990 and 1999, and 279 between 2000 and 2014.[5] Of these 1,834 marriages, we count 454 men and 309 women born in Morocco. If we consider the category "Sephardic" to include people born abroad or in Canada, we count 831 Sephardic men and 668 Sephardic women.[6]

Overall, the number of marriages celebrated in the synagogues in our study increased over the years, with a decrease only in the period 1969–1989. The Île-de-France sample is composed of 2,126 marriage certificates from a variety of synagogues located in Paris and the surrounding area between 1961 and 1975. The presence of people from Morocco in the sample is a consequence of the fact that there are 1,063 records in which at least one of the spouses was born in that country—a total of 561 men and 571 women.

---

[5] Data for the years 2008, 2009, and 2011 are missing.
[6] Charles Shahar (2015, 49) defines people as Sephardic if they were born in Afghanistan, Albania, Algeria, Bulgaria, Egypt, France, Greece, India, Iran, Iraq, Jordan, Kuwait, Lebanon, Libya, Morocco, North Yemen, Pakistan, Portugal, Saudi Arabia, South Yemen, Spain, Syria, Tunisia, Turkey, Yemen, or Yugoslavia (Bosnia and Herzegovina, Croatia, Kosovo, Macedonia, Montenegro, Serbia and Slovenia); if their mother and father were born in those countries; if their mother tongue is French, Arabic, Greek, Bulgarian, or one of the Yugoslavian languages; or if they are children in a household where both parents fit these criteria.

Who Do Moroccan Jews Marry?

Previous work established that 67 percent of the marriages that took place at the consistorial synagogue on rue des Tournelles were between North African Jews. This figure compares to 11 percent at the rue Copernic synagogue and 18 percent at the Spanish and Portuguese Synagogue in Montreal (Cohen and Scioldo-Zürcher 2014). The collection of additional data in other Parisian consistorial synagogues and the study of marriages after the 1980s suggest about the same level of geographical in-marriage as in previous work among Moroccan natives in liberal synagogues and a small increase in in-marriage in the Parisian consistorial synagogues and Montreal.

For the Paris region, the most common union among North African Jews was between Moroccans and Algerians (40 percent), followed by Moroccans among themselves (29 percent). The latter percentage is almost ten percentage points higher than in earlier studies. In the case of Montreal's Spanish and Portuguese Synagogue and Or Hahayim, the extension of collection dates does not change the results; unions between Moroccans compose fully 90 percent of North African marriages. However, among Moroccan, most marriages are between Moroccans and Canadians (220 marriages compared to 177 marriages between Moroccans). For 30 percent of marriages of men with Canadians, the fiancées are French Canadians who converted from Catholicism to Judaism (Cohen and Guerry 2011). In Paris, there were 256 marriages between individuals born in Morocco and France, which attests to the integration of newcomers into the host society, since this figure is higher than the number of marriages between Moroccan.

These data show that living in Montreal or Paris is associated with relative openness in terms of choice of spouse. But if marriage to non-Moroccans is frequent, even the majority, in the two areas studied, small disparities exist between men and women. In Montreal, 61 percent of Moroccan-born men married women who were not born in Morocco. For Moroccan-born women the comparable figure is 58 percent. The situation is similar in the Paris region, where marriage between the Moroccan-born is common, but not the majority. Some 68 percent of Moroccan-born men married non-Moroccan women, compared to 64 percent of Moroccan-born women. Thus, somewhat greater openness to geographical out-marriage is evident in Montreal and among men. Still, members of this first cohort of migrants, both men and women, tended to marry outside of their group of origin, while retaining their strong identification with Judaism by converting their mostly Catholic fiancées to their own faith.

Occupational Profile of Moroccan Jews in Montreal and Paris

Marriage records also allow us to assess the socio-occupational situation of the migrant populations at the time of their arrival in the two cities. Analysis of these data allows us not only to draw comparisons between the migrations to Canada and France, but also to propose avenues for drawing comparisons within these Jewish communities. The Canadian classification that we have adopted is particularly broad and is mainly concerned with the economic sector, not hierarchical position. Applying this classification allows us to conclude that the occupational profiles of Moroccan Jews who married in Montreal are similar to those of the rest of Canada, as are the occupational profiles of Moroccan Jews who married in Montreal compared to those in the Paris area. However, the Montreal and Paris samples themselves differ somewhat. Notably, the sample from the Montreal synagogues consists of 418 men and 273 women (a gender ratio of 1.5), while the sample from the Paris area synagogues consists of 573 men and 474 women (a gender ratio of 1.2).

For native Moroccans, the main occupations in Paris are in "sales and services" (126 people) and "business, finance, and administration" (119 people). Students and people in scientific occupations come next, with 87 and 75 people, respectively. The "sales and services" category includes a wide range of occupations associated with sales, but also with craft skills, while the "business, finance, and administration" category also includes some management positions. Technical occupations are included in the "trades, transportation, machinery, and related" and "manufacturing and public utilities" categories. They include workers at various skill levels. The occupational structure of married men associated with the Montreal synagogues is similar to that of the men living in Paris. In the two Montreal synagogues, most of the men are in "sales and services," "business, finance, and administration," and "trades, transportation, machinery, and related" occupations.

However, an analysis within the main categories reveals a difference between the two populations. If "sales and service" personnel are most numerous in both cases, they include a different mix of occupations in the two cities. In Montreal, the largest group in this category, at 46 percent, is in sales, while the comparable figure in Paris is 21 percent. Meanwhile, the percentage of craft workers and those involved in commerce is higher in Paris. Comparing Montreal fiancés born in Morocco with those not born in Morocco also reinforces the idea of a relative concentration of Moroccan natives in the "sales and services" category.

At the time of their marriage in Montreal, 82 percent of Moroccan-born women had a paying job.[7] This was not the case in the period immediately following their arrival in Montreal, as the JIAS data show. In fact, their labour-force participation rate is nearly the same as that of Canadian-born women (83 percent) and considerably higher than that of women in Canada who were born in a country other than Canada or Morocco (76 percent).

The occupational profile of women born in Montreal is dominated by two main categories: "administrative occupations" (28 percent) and "sales occupations" (27 percent), the latter of which also includes some occupations associated with craft work, such as hairdressing. Native Moroccan fiancées are more likely to belong to the latter category than are brides born in other countries, testifying to the relative ease of entry into hairdressing.

This is less the case in the Paris sample, where the concentration is higher in "business, finance, and administration" (49 percent) and the "student" group (20 percent). The first group includes secretaries and stenographers/typists, the most common occupations. In this respect, the concentration of women in Paris in these professions as well as in Montreal sheds light on the process of entry into the labour market, which was made possible in the occupations associated with secretarial work by the fact that this young and educated population either attended francophone schools in Morocco or had been educated in the host country. In France, these jobs are often the first entry point into the labour market.

Finally, we can consider the place of students in comparing the Montreal and Paris samples. The percentage of female students was higher in Paris (20 percent) than in Montreal (16 percent). The latter was close to the percentage of non-Moroccan women who married in the Montreal sample (17 percent). The discrepancy between male students in Paris (13 percent) and Montreal (3 percent) was more substantial.

It is difficult to interpret this important Montreal/Paris difference. It can be considered on two levels. First, it may reflect the relative ease

---

[7] The percentage without a paying job is calculated from mentions of "housewife" and "unemployed" and the absence of any indication that the individual was in the paid labour force.

of access to higher education in Paris for a migrant population, schooled in French, in a context where it is difficult for them to find a job and where tuition is free. Second, it may reflect greater confidence among the Parisians that their entry into the paid labour force will be relatively easy after they complete their studies. The fact that the absence of a permanent job does not seem to be an obstacle in some students' decision to marry in Paris supports the latter interpretation.

Upward Mobility and Career Paths

It is difficult to discern much upward mobility for men over the years, but upward mobility is more apparent for women (see Table 3.2 for men and Table 3.3 for women). The decade-by-decade figures in Table 3.2 and Table 3.3 should be read with caution, since the number of people per decade varies substantially.

Table 3.2. Occupational distribution of Moroccan-Jewish men in Montreal (1969–2014, percentage)

	1969–1979	1980–1989	1990–1999	2000–2014	Total
Sales and services	33	22	27	25	28
Business, fnance, and administration	10	23	20	13	16
Trades, transportation, machinery, and related	14	11	16	8	13
Management	13	13	10	13	13
Education, law, and social, community, and government services	6	8	8	13	7
Natural and applied sciences and related	8	5	4	13	7
Arts, culture, sports, and recreation	7	7	0	0	6
Health	3	5	6	13	5
Students	5	1	2	0	0
Manufacturing and public utilities	1	4	4	0	2
Retired	0	1	2	4	1
Total	100	100	99	102	98
Number of cases	197	148	49	24	418

Note: Some columns do not equal 100 due to rounding.
Sources: Marriage records, Spanish and Portuguese Synagogue and Or Hahayim Synagogue.

Nevertheless, we can see meaningful change over time. The percentage of men in "sales and services" dropped eight percentage points between the 1970s and the 2000s. For occupations in "arts, culture, sports, and recreation," the absolute number of individuals is small, but the decline is seven percentage points between the 1970s and the 2000s. For students, we see a five percentage-point decline over the same period, likely due to the fact that the average age at marriage increased over time and the fact that men who marry do so after their studies. On the other hand, the percentage of individuals in the health field grew by ten points over the period under consideration. Although a total of just twenty people were in the health professions over the entire period, the relative importance of these occupations in the workforce may reflect an increase in professional qualifications overall.

For women, the tendency towards increased professional qualifications is more conspicuous. The professional profile of Moroccan-born women changed over the years. The proportion of women in "business, finance, and administration" fell by nineteen percentage points while the corresponding figure for students was seventeen percentage points. Sales and hairdressing were common occupations in the female population in the 1970s, but the number of hairdressers, for example, fell from twenty-three in the 1970s to ten in the 1980s and then to zero in the 1990s.

Table 3.3. Occupational distribution of Moroccan-Jewish women in Montreal (1969–2014, percentage).

	1969–1979	1980–1989	1990–1999	2000–2014	Total
Business, fnance, and administration	36	23	18	10	27
Sales and services	28	28	25	19	27
Students	17	22	11	0	16
Education, law, and social, community, and government services	9	11	14	33	12
Health	4	2	29	19	7
Management	4	4	0	14	4
Arts, culture, sports, and recreation	1	2	4	0	1
Manufacturing and public utilities	0	5	0	0	1
Natural and applied sciences and related	1	2	0	0	1
Trades, transportation, machinery, and related	1	0	0	5	1
Pensioners	0	0	0	0	0
Total	101	99	101	100	97
Number of cases	142	82	28	21	273

Note: Some columns do not equal 100 due to rounding.

Sources: Marriage records, Spanish and Portuguese Synagogue and Or Hahayim Synagogue.

On the other hand, employment in "education, law, and social, community, and government services" rose from 9 percent (thirteen people) in the 1970s to 33 percent (seven people) in the 2000s. Similarly, even though the number of women in the health professions remains modest, it increased between 1970 and 1990 from five to eight people. On the whole, it seems clear that women have improved their professional qualifications over time, partly because of their improved integration into Canadian society and partly because of the rising status of all women in Canadian society over the nearly half-century represented by Table 3.3.

In the first years after immigration, some Moroccan Jews experienced difficulties integrating into Montreal's paid labour force. However, their descendants appear to have experienced considerable upward mobility.

Women apparently had more difficulty entering the paid labour force than men did, probably because of the way the work world was structured and the greater emphasis placed on men's work. It is also possible that immigration tightened the family sphere, initially distancing women from paid work. This issue requires more research, especially through the use of surveys and oral histories. Over time, constraints on women's labour force participation faded. The labour force participation rate for women increased the longer families had to adjust to their new country, the longer the presence of women in the paid labour force normalized their taking on paid work, and the larger the proportion of women who attended school in Canada.

The occupational profile of native Moroccans who marry in the Paris region and in Montreal are similar, but not identical. For instance, there have been more students among Moroccan Jews in Paris and more salespeople in Montreal. Improved qualifications and consequent upward mobility have been evident from the beginning of Moroccan-Jewish immigration in Montreal, especially for women of the second generation. Immigration has also enabled Moroccan Canadians to out-marry geographically, socially, and even religiously, although women are less likely than men to do so. The results of this survey therefore suggest that marriage strategies reflect a generally positive outlook, especially among men, on the host society. However, it is the acquisition of professional qualifications that allows for upward mobility, especially for women.

CHAPTER 4

Sephardi Jews in Montreal

Yolande Cohen

Montreal, a metropolis of some three million inhabitants, is home to a large and diverse Jewish community (Cohen 2013). More than a quarter of that community is Sephardic. Who would have thought that the descendants of Jews forced to leave Spain by the Inquisition would make their homes in Montreal, giving birth to a multi-ethnic Sephardic community whose existence in the twenty-first century is a sign of its durability and adaptability. Where did these Sephardim come from? How did they arrive in Montreal? How can they be identified today? These are the principal questions that must be asked concerning these migrants as we retrace the highlights of their journey from the four corners of the earth.

A Two-Thousand-Year History

Sephardic communities look back on a tumultuous history marked by numerous migrations as well as long periods of settlement. The name *Sepharad*, from Hebrew, has been used by Jews since the fifth century CE to designate Spain. By extension, it came to refer to Spain's Jewish inhabitants. With the expulsions of the Jews of Spain and Portugal by their Christian monarchs in 1492 and 1497, the Jews of the Iberian Peninsula emigrated in large part to North Africa, where they created a community distinct in its origins and customs. The Sephardic exiles were called *Megorashim* (the exiles) to distinguish them from the native North African Jews, who were called *Toshavim* (the natives). Those Jews who decided to remain in the now-Christian Iberian Peninsula were forced to deny their Jewish faith and convert to Christianity. These *conversos*, some of whom continued the secret practice of Judaism, were considered by many to be crypto-Jews, and were sometimes called *Marranos*. The expulsion from Spain, on the one hand, and the phenomenon of Marranism, on the other, became basic building blocks of Sephardic identity. In early modern times, one could find Sephardic Jews settled in places like North Africa, the Netherlands, Great Britain, Turkey, and the Balkans.

The First Sephardic Migration to Montreal

It is from this early modern Sephardic diaspora that a handful of British Jews of Spanish and Portuguese origins came to Montreal and, in 1768, founded Shearith Israel, the Spanish and Portuguese Congregation, one of the oldest synagogues in North America and the first in Canada. This orthodox Sephardic synagogue has maintained its existence until the present day.

The arrival in Montreal of massive numbers of Ashkenazi Jewish refugees from Eastern Europe at the beginning of the twentieth century permanently changed the composition and structure of Montreal's Jewish community. In that era, the community acquired a number of essential welfare institutions, like the Jewish Immigrant Aid Services (JIAS), which helped in the absorption of immigrants, and a network of synagogues and schools for the maintenance of religious practice.

Because of this Eastern-European Jewish influx, the Sephardi community in Montreal diminished in relative importance, if not in prestige. Additionally, beyond the original Sephardi families, the Spanish and Portuguese Synagogue attracted a number of Ashkenazi members. Thus, the Sephardi tradition in Montreal experienced a certain diminution, without, however, disappearing completely.

Sephardi Migration after the Second World War

With the end of the Second World War, the creation of the State of Israel in 1948, and the decolonization of North Africa, the history of the Jews of the Maghreb came to a turning point. The situation in North African countries became more and more problematic for Jews, while the question of aid for the Jewish community in the Arab countries (Maghreb) already an issue in the nineteenth century, became an urgent reality.[1]

There is a large body of recent scholarship on the nature of and the principal factors for the massive exodus of Jews from the Arab countries in the mid-twentieth century. What was the nature of discrimination against and the persecution of Jews in this time and place? What was the role of the State of Israel? What was the role played by international Jewish organizations in this migration? Certain leaders of world Jewry helped to organize the Jews' departure, while others put into motion policies seeking to ameliorate the Jews' situations in their homelands by financing Jewish institutions in North Africa, for instance. Other complex questions arise concerning the immediate reception of the Jewish emigrants in Israel, France, and Canada.

Some of these Sephardi migrants understood their journey as repatriation. This was true for Jews from Algeria, as well as for those Tunisian and Moroccan Jews who possessed French citizenship. At times, Jewish emigration was seen as the political exclusion of Jews on the part of newly independent Arab states, and at other times it was viewed as an outright expulsion, particularly in the cases of Egypt and Iraq. Sometimes the departure could be seen as a voluntary choice; at other times it was understood as an exile. These conflicting interpretations, to which various political and administrative problems are linked, are as complex as they are intertwined. It remains difficult to comprehend the hierarchy of individual and collective decisions that drove individuals and families to depart their native countries with no great hope of return.

In the case of Israel, and also Canada, the Jews of North Africa and of the *Machrek* were considered by some governments and international Jewish organizations as contributing to the population of their countries. For those among the emigrants who possessed French citizenship, destinations were largely determined by the legal obligations of France to its citizens in Algeria after its independence. Others wished to make the best of the situation, and sought greater security, or followed economic and, indeed, religious imperatives.

---

[1] *Maghreb* refers to northwest Africa, west of Egypt, and *Machrek*, referring to Arab countries to the east of Egypt and north of the Arabian Peninsula, i.e., Iraq, Palestine, Jordan, Kuwait, Lebanon, and Syria.

It is from Morocco, which became independent in 1956, that approximately 15,000 Jews came to Montreal. About 80 percent of Moroccan-Jewish emigrants went to Israel in several waves that ended in the 1970s. Several thousand Moroccan Jews left their country for France and Canada during the last major wave, which lasted from the end of the 1960s through the 1970s. However, this schema does not exclude the indirect routes by which some Moroccan-born Jews, having tried life in Israel or France, later came to Canada.

The arrival of Sephardi Jews in Montreal enables us to study their means of adaptation and incorporation as well as the transformation of the community in their new host country. This study of the integration of this group in Montreal may be considered a model of this genre, not only for diaspora studies, but also for studies devoted to migration. These Jews integrated into an older, established Jewish community and transformed it.

A Multi-Ethnic Jewish Community: Institutions and Policies of Absorption

The arrival in Montreal of Holocaust refugees marked a turning point in the life of the Montreal-Jewish community and helped it emerge in the postwar period as a major international Jewish centre. The arrival of Jews forced out of Iraq after Israel's independence in 1948, as well as that of the Moroccan Jews, also made its mark on the dynamic of the Montreal-Jewish community. Beyond the issues intrinsic to the departure of the Jews from their homeland, we need to add factors stemming from the nature of the Montreal-Jewish community as well as from Canadian immigration policy.

The Jewish community in Canada had acquired a considerable role as an intervener with the Canadian federal government on questions of Jewish immigration since the 1920s. The JIAS, mentioned above, had developed a number of services for newly arrived Jews. In the postwar period, the Jewish community was concerned about its future: Its leaders had commissioned internal reports that forecasted the rapid aging of the Jewish population. Thus, they naturally sought to increase the pool of Jewish immigrants coming to Canada. When Canada liberalized its immigration policy, the Jewish community was ready with an efficient network of institutions to welcome new arrivals. For its part, the Quebec government understood the importance of controlling the selection of immigrants and of providing itself with the authority to accomplish this goal. The Quebec Ministry of Immigration was thus created in 1968. Knowledge of French at this time became a much more important factor in the point system for immigrants seeking visas to immigrate to Quebec.[2]

This combination of factors was favourable for the immigration of French-speaking Jews from the Maghreb. Many of them arrived with the aid of JIAS and were given further help by the Jewish Vocational Services (JVS). It was thus a Montreal-Jewish community that was exceedingly well organized into which these Jews arriving from Muslim Arab countries sought to integrate. The Jewish community of Montreal up to that point had been mostly English-speaking, and it sought to find the means to integrate these French-speaking newcomers, even if it was not necessarily prepared to make room for their religious rituals and cultural traditions. For their part, the new immigrants did not really think of themselves as a homogenous group. They continued to see themselves in the identities they had constructed over the course of centuries in their respective homelands, and they thus set to work to create schools and synagogues, as well as cultural and recreational centres, which would attract other people who were also from their countries. The special role that was played by the Spanish and Portuguese congregation in the absorption of these immigrants needs to be emphasized. It was in the context of that synagogue that the first encounters took place between Montreal's "old" and "new" Sephardim. The congregation's longstanding identification with the Sephardi tradition attracted newcomers who celebrated their marriages there in the early years and encountered other Jews, including Sephardim of different origins as well as Ashkenazim. In the 1960s, the Spanish and Portuguese Synagogue, which had been preponderantly English-speaking and Ashkenazi, became an important meeting place for Moroccan Jews. It was also in the framework of this synagogue that the new immigrants worked out a means of identifying with Sephardi Judaism in Montreal, which gave them the advantage of integrating into an existing, recognized, and respected community, while at the same time asserting a common identity that did not specifically bind them to their country of origin. Thus, the Iraqi and

---

[2] It was in 1967 that Canada adopted a point system for the selection of immigrants based on objective criteria, such as education and family reunification, replacing previous criteria, which included ethnic origin, colour, and religion, and were overtly discriminatory.

Egyptian Jewish immigrants who found themselves members of the Spanish and Portuguese Synagogue coexisted in a noisy multi-ethnic crucible. Each group wished to impose its special liturgy, traditions, and melodies on the congregation. After the arrival of a large number of Moroccan-Jewish immigrants, a reinvented Sephardi identity began combining a number of new and old religious and cultural practices, causing Sephardi identity to undergo unexpected development in Montreal. The Spanish and Portuguese Synagogue in those years played a crucial role, despite the fact that after 1970 the Moroccan Jews were numerous enough to celebrate their marriages at another community institution, the Shomrim Laboker Congregation, as well. The recruitment of Salomon Amzallag (Samy el Maghribi), who had been a well-known musician and popular singer in Morocco, to be hazzan at the Spanish and Portuguese Synagogue from 1968 to 1984, also attracted Moroccan Jews to this synagogue. Later, in the 1980s, with the establishment of other Sephardi congregations, the importance of the Spanish and Portuguese Synagogue diminished.

The development of a hybrid Sephardi identity occurred in both Israel and the diaspora. However, Montreal witnessed this hybridization of different versions of Sephardism within a specifically Canadian context—that of Canadian multiculturalism. Jews of the Maghreb and Machrek who participated in the great post-colonial migrations of the latter half of the twentieth century thus contributed to the diversity of Montreal-Jewish identity by creating their own version of an identity and a culture that had already been present in Montreal. To Montreal-Jewish identity and culture, they added the dimension of an oriental Judaism that flourished on the banks of the St. Lawrence in the midst of a greater Jewish community.

In analyzing the institutional structure of this group of Jews from Arab countries, we can discern how Sephardi identity is constructed in the context of a larger Jewish community.

The Structure of the Sephardi Community: From the Groupement juif nord-africain to the Communauté sépharade unifiée du Québec (CSUQ)

Of the new Jewish immigrants who settled in Quebec after 1960, Jews from Morocco constituted the largest "national" group. They numbered 7,995 persons who arrived from 1960–1991 (according to the 1991 census). That is nearly double the number of Jewish immigrants to

Canada from Poland (4,250), and much more than the number of Jews originating in all other countries (including France and Israel). It is thus not astonishing that it was this community that had the largest impact on the construction of a Sephardic identity in Montreal. The arrival of a great number of Moroccan Jews, the bulk of whom arrived in a span of less than twenty years, changed the balance of the different ethnic or national communities that make up the Jewish community of Montreal, whose population now is nearly 90,000.

While JIAS, the agency that aided the immigration of North African Jews to Montreal, had the responsibility of getting them established at the beginning, it quickly clashed with the new immigrants' desire to establish separate institutions. Thus, in 1959 the Association juive nord-africaine, which soon changed its name to Groupement juif nord-africain, declared its intention to respond to the cultural and religious needs of its own constituency. After the demise of that institution, the Fédération sépharade des juifs de langue française was founded in 1965 and became, in 1966, the Association sépharade francophone.

It is significant to note that the term *North African* was dropped, and its place was taken by the ancient and mythic Sephardi identity, which allowed these immigrants to assert their identity in the face of the English-speaking Jewish community. We can clearly see the two principles upon which the differentiation was constructed: the Sephardi heritage (old) and loyalty to the French language (new). After the arrival of large numbers of Moroccan Jews in the 1970s, the need to create their own Sephardi synagogues and community centres was felt in all the different neighbourhoods in which they lived.[3] North African Jews also negotiated with the Young Men's Hebrew Association (YMHA) to create a French-speaking group for young people and a French-speaking adult group, later adding one for young adults. In 1971, this became the Centre communautaire juif (CCJ). More than simply a leisure centre, the CCJ offers socio-cultural and recreation

---

[3] Congregation Or Hahayim of Côte Saint-Luc was founded in 1972, and its synagogue dedicated in 1981. A Sephardic community was founded in Laval in 1972, and its synagogue, Or Sepharade, was dedicated in 1980. In Ville Saint-Laurent, Petah Tikva was created in 1973 and its building dedicated in 1983. Another Sephardic congregation, Hekhal Shalom, was founded in Ville Saint-Laurent in 1981. The Sephardic Association of the West Island was created in 1975 and has recently acquired a community centre, which also serves as a synagogue.

activities specifically directed toward Sephardim, with departments for children, adolescents, young adults, and golden age adults, focusing on leisure, culture, and religion. It also houses a synagogue and a nursery school, which are frequented by many Sephardim.

The Communauté sépharade du Québec (CSQ), created in 1976, immediately demonstrated its divergence from the institutions of the Ashkenazi-Jewish community, while independent institutions, mainly synagogues, continued to function outside its auspices. The main objectives of the CSQ are to preserve and promote Sephardi culture and to contribute to a better integration of the immigrants in their host country. Just like similar institutions in Morocco, it has divisions that deal with religious matters (such as registers of marital status, associations for visiting the sick, and the Hevra Kadisha [burial society]), social assistance (such as providing information on social services and linking clients to agencies that can respond to their issues), and the dissemination of information through a journal (*La voix sépharade*). It also offers direct services to its members in the critical areas of education and welfare. The CSQ merged with the CCJ in 2001 to create the Communauté sépharade unifiée du Québec (CSUQ).

In the area of education, the creation of École Maïmonide in 1969 was an important event in the growth of the community. This school offers primary and secondary education supervised by the Quebec Ministry of Education, as well as a program of Judaic studies geared toward preserving and reinforcing the Jewish-Moroccan heritage. It has enjoyed unprecedented success. Its three campuses serve the three principal neighbourhoods in which Sephardim live. One of the buildings in its campus in Saint-Laurent has been named in honour of Mohammed V, king of Morocco. Another Sephardi school, created in 1976 and affiliated with the Alliance israélite universelle (AIU), testifies to the relationship with the French Jewish educational institution, in which many of the Montreal schools teachers were trained.

Lastly, the Centre Hillel was created in 1972. It is a French-speaking branch of Montreal's B'nai B'rith Hillel Foundation and serves French-speaking students at the postsecondary level (college and university). Students at the Université de Montréal who are affiliated with Centre Hillel publish a journal, *Bleu-Blanc,* which has had a long run. There are over a dozen groups of lesser size that also cater to Sephardim. The multiplicity of these cultural and religious groups reflects the profound nature of the roots this community has put down, as well as the eagerness of its members, who think that communal organization is indispensable to maintaining their identity.

In the areas of art and culture, most Moroccan-Jewish groups sponsor lectures with local or out-of-town speakers, especially during the Festival Sépharade or Jewish Book Month. During these events, Quebec society has a chance to become more aware of the contributions of the Jewish-Moroccan community.

A small group of committed young people participated in the creation of these institutions. As is the case in other communities in Quebec, the leaders of community organizations are mostly men between the ages of 45 and 60 whose occupation is either business or education. These leaders also took the initiative in 1990 to create the Congrès Sépharade du Canada, to develop links with Sephardi communities in the rest of Canada and to have representation of the CSQ locally and internationally, particularly with respect to Israel. The CSQ is also affiliated with the Rassemblement du Judaïsme Marocain.

This strong institutionalization, achieved by a group of motivated leaders, needs to be understood in the context of a Quebec and Canadian immigration policy that supports the recognition and maintenance of the original cultures of immigrants. These institutions have also permitted Moroccan Jews, despite the secular identity of many, to continue the practice of a traditional Judaism and to support a rich liturgical heritage. The Sephardi community structure, which supports its members from cradle to grave and offers an extremely varied range of services with its synagogues, schools, welfare organizations, and cemeteries, structures its identity and mediates the community's relations with other Canadians and Québécois.

In the 1970s and 1980s, it was possible to speak of Sephardi-Ashkenazi tension within the Montreal-Jewish community and to explain the high rate of intermarriages between Sephardim and Catholic Quebec women as a result of Ashkenazi hostility to Sephardim, who were considered by them to be lower class and possessing neither culture nor education. Now, however, Montreal Jews feel that their community has been created anew with multiple components.

Indeed, the Sephardi community is an integral part of this new image of Montreal Jewry in the context of the Montreal "Jewish campus" where all the major institutions of the Jewish community have been concentrated since the 1990s, including the CCJ, Gelber Centre, Segal Centre, etc. The Spanish and Portuguese Synagogue, which was completely renovated in recent years, has also re-established its pride of place as the oldest synagogue in Montreal and one of the oldest in North America.

This process of settlement, which has occupied three generations of immigrants in Montreal since the end of the 1960s, has had many phases. It must be understood as an exemplary case of the capacity of immigrants to reduce barriers, whether real or perceived, between themselves and their host societies in a post-colonial context. From images of the Jewish pariah, rebel or newly established, described so well by Hannah Arendt, we pass imperceptibly to images of Jews as figures of nostalgia (blending in an ahistorical setting). Sephardi Judaism, disoriented by the exile of most of its indigenous communities, ill-treated and disrespected in Israel, discovered in its Canadian diaspora an institutional completeness that it had lost with its migrations. These Montreal-Sephardi struggles have resulted in a very strong effort to maintain community traditions, especially those having to do with religion and food. Unless these traditions are ultimately reduced to folklore (a fate that threatens all minority cultures), they can become means for the genuine affirmation of an identity that is both hybrid and open.

The Socio-Economic Characteristics of the Sephardi Community

Today, the Montreal Sephardi community is more than 20,000 strong. It is a religious and ethnic group that is well integrated into the cosmopolitan city of Montreal both economically and socially.[4]

First of all, just over 40 percent of this population has at this point been born in Canada, while 34 percent was born in Morocco and the rest in France (5.6 percent), Israel (5.5 percent), Egypt (3 percent), Iraq (2.2 percent), Western Europe (2 percent), Eastern Europe (1.6 percent), and elsewhere (such as Lebanon, Turkey, United States, South America). This proportion of immigrants in the Sephardi community (59.6 percent) is high in comparison with the more established Ashkenazi population. The recent immigration of this population (of which one third originated in Morocco, and most of which has been in Canada for fewer than thirty years) explains this high proportion of immigrants. It is

---

[4] Sephardim are not only found in Montreal. The 2001 census found 8,070 Sephardi Jews in Toronto (making up 24.7 percent of the Canadian Sephardic population) and 870 in Vancouver (2.7 percent).

rather the 40 percent born in Canada who consider themselves to be Sephardi that might seem to be high. The number of Catholic women who converted to Judaism prior to their marriages partly explains the relatively high proportion of Sephardi Jews born in Canada.

The geographic location of the Sephardim in Montreal is similar to the residential patterns of the Jewish community in Montreal as a whole. Thus, a strong majority of them moved into traditionally Jewish neighbourhoods in the west of Montreal: Côte Saint-Luc (4,285), Saint-Laurent (3,770), Snowdon (2,295), Côte-des-Neiges (1,715), and the West Island (2,185). Only 1,785 of them live elsewhere (Verdun, Lasalle, Lachine, etc.). Saint-Laurent has the highest proportion of Sephardim to the total Jewish population (45.8 percent).

The majority of Sephardim live as couples (77.4 percent), even though only 45.5 percent of them are married (the rate of marriage for Montreal as a whole is 33.2 percent). Thus, the great majority of children (89 percent) live in a two-parent family. It is a young population that is 80 percent French-speaking, though 26.5 percent also speak English at home. Other traditional languages, like Judeo-Arabic, Hebrew, and Spanish, have seen a considerable decline. The educational level of the Sephardim is comparable to that of the Ashkenazi group. 43 percent of Sephardim have finished secondary school; 21.4 percent have a college diploma or professional certificate; 22.6 percent have a bachelor's degree; 11.2 percent have a master's degree; and 2.8 percent have a doctorate or medical degree. Thus, more than one third of the Sephardim in Montreal (35.7 percent) possess a university degree. This is comparable to the Jewish community as a whole, but higher than the population of Montreal (21.5 percent of the Montreal population has a university degree). This indicates that the Sephardim have made an important investment in education as a mode of integration into the Quebec and North American environment. The great majority of its members are mostly young people and adults of working age (26 percent are 25–44 and 27 percent are 45–64), with 15.5 percent over 65. These results from the 2001 census confirm the results of the first studies devoted to these new immigrants since the 1970s, which spoke of their successful economic integration.

The majority of Sephardim are professionals (16.2 percent), upper and intermediate level managers (14.1 percent), sales and service personnel (12.6 percent), secretarial and office employees (9 percent), and technical and paraprofessionals (7.8 percent). Their contributions to the economic life of the metropolis are made primarily in the textile, clothing, shoe, and hairdressing industries. There is also a significant number of them in the liberal professions and on the staff of parapublic institutions in health, social services, and education on the primary, secondary, college, and university levels. Their salary structure reflects their median status (defined as between $10,000 and $24,000), with a median income of $23,268, which is somewhat larger than the Montreal average and a bit lower than that of Ashkenazi Jews. More precisely, one quarter of Sephardim earn less than $10,000 a year, approximately 30 percent earn between $10,000 and $25,000, and the rest are about equally divided at 17 percent for both the $40,000–$70,000 and the $70,000–$100,000 groups. Only 5.2 percent earn more than $100,000. While 82 percent of this population live above the poverty line, with an overrepresentation of business and professional workers (30.3 percent), 17.8 percent, mostly seniors, live below the poverty line.

The Sephardi population is slowly increasing and is generally well integrated economically. It has demonstrated a remarkable adaptability to the social and cultural context of Quebec. It has succeeded in establishing a certain societal visibility and has made its presence and unique identity known in various ways, thus changing the image of the Montreal-Jewish community.

Culturally, Moroccan Jews in Montreal are in a special position with respect to their integration into Montreal's society. Because of their Jewishness, they share many things with the Ashkenazim. However, the Ashkenazi community, due to the number of its members, its predominant use of English, its economic power, and its well-developed network of communal institutions, desired to integrate these new immigrants as speedily as possible, without consideration of their identity and their knowledge of French. Furthermore, the processes by which this renewed Sephardi identity was established are equally important to establish. It is important to take careful note of the periodization of this process, because it coincides with the development of demands for the affirmation of French in Quebec.

Moreover, the arrival of these French-speaking Jews in Quebec allowed certain Quebec scholars to advance the possibility of a convergence between the Jewish minority and that of French Quebec, thus engendering the interculturalism advocated by Gérard Bouchard. There are some weaknesses in this analysis: the French-Canadians are not a minority but a majority in Quebec, and the antisemitism that exists in Quebec, as it does in Canada as a whole, does not allow the convergence that Bouchard hoped for with the Jewish community. On the contrary, Ignaki Olazabal's study presents the paradoxical situation of a Jewish community that is strong and alive, but relatively withdrawn within itself as a result of a "mis encounter" with the majority society (using the terminology of Zygmunt Bauman). Will Montreal's several solitudes ultimately overwhelm this small group of French-speaking Jews?

The social and economic integration of the Sephardim of Quebec has indeed been accomplished seemingly without great clashes, helped by the existence of strong communal structures, which also permitted the emergence of a social stratum that is well-to-do and can be found in some beautiful upscale neighbourhoods. In many respects, we may also say that the Sephardim have created their own identity, which involves adherence to Jewishness, Frenchness, and the heritage of Sepharad. The most important of these factors remains religion, which is supported by synagogues, families, and community schools. Language plays an equally determining role in the community's interaction with Quebec society, even though its use of English as well as French demonstrates its willingness to integrate into a greater North American environment beyond that of Quebec.

This is a portrait of the Jewish-Moroccan presence in Quebec today. There has been a good socio-economic integration of the community, along with retention and maintenance of the community's religious character as a marker of its identity. Nonetheless, we must add that the notion of *Sephardisme* has a complex and somewhat paradoxical character. Thus, members of this group sometimes identify with Morocco, sometimes with Israel, sometimes with France. Their complex ties and history, which have been radically cut off given the conditions of their departure and their arrival, appear vaguely under the smooth surface of the statistics. Other elements contributing to the interpretation of their recent history might possibly reside in the unstated (stifled) and practically unthought (traumatic) accounts of their migrations.

PART III

Memoirs of Migration in Canada

CHAPTER 5

Memories of Departures: Stories of Jews from Muslim Lands in Montreal

Yolande Cohen, Martin Messika, and Sara Cohen Fournier

> Yolande Cohen: *What we could start with, like we usually do: you could tell us where and when you were born, and a bit of the conditions of life in Algeria, and then we will talk about your departures. Maybe we can start like this if it works for you.*
> Jean: *Oh for the departures, that is quite a euphemism, eh…*

An oral history interview is an encounter between two individuals around a chosen theme (Cohen, Messika, and Cohen Fournier 2015).[1] Interviewer and interviewee come together to meet an idea. The encounter with this idea can feel unexpected or arise in conflict. Or it can feel normal and almost awaited. In the passage quoted above, Yolande Cohen starts by outlining for the interviewee an expected course. Jean's immediate reaction is to proclaim his own understanding of the word *departures*. Reactions differ between interviewees, or from collective frameworks that have shaped

---

[1] We want to thank Steven High for his kind and steady support; Hubert Villeneuve and Jared Conrad-Bradshaw, who had the difficult task of revising our English. Our thanks go also to Linda Guerry, Myriam Chebat, and Antoine Burgard for their contribution, dedication, and work in our research team.

individual's perspectives. Yet underlying historical context gives us clues to probe various meanings around specific outcomes. In this context, Jean is a man in his sixties reflecting on his life, a life that has brought him to leave Algeria, the first of his many departures:

> Jean: I left um [...] in secret, and [cough] without telling my neighbours. My parents told me: "And above all, you do not tell anyone, huh, you shut up [...] you shut up." I had a great friend, an old childhood friend, when I was young; his name was Boris, who lives in Haifa today, well in the suburbs of Haifa. My parents said: "Especially, do not tell Boris." So I didn't tell Boris, and it hurt so much to leave without saying goodbye. So I left [...] I left like a thief [from] my parents' house. We lived in an alley, and my dad backed up the car just in front of the house, and when he arrived at the door [cough], he opened the trunk and said: "Get in." I got in the trunk, and I did part of the trip in the trunk. When we were far enough, he opened the trunk, and I got out. He brought me to the airport.

Our questions, inserted within the scope of departures, reflect the plurality of voices present within a given community of Jews that once lived in Arab-Muslim countries and have settled, sometimes temporarily, in Montreal. What are the circumstances that have led Jean to feel that the word *departures*, which we used to describe our project was ill adequate to encompass his own experience? He reacted strongly, showing us that for him departure meant expulsion, an unpleasant expression. Interviewing Sephardic Jews living in Montreal raised the question of the memories of those departures and of the trauma surrounding them. Not all narratives were embedded in trauma, on the contrary, many interviewees understood and presented their departures in a context of easiness and simplicity, as will be explained in this chapter. We sought to bring the wide variety of perspectives on this high level of migration from Arab-Muslim countries.

In this chapter, we raise the question of how Sephardic Jews coming from Arab-Muslim countries have depicted their own departure, which was considered by some as a forced exile. What types of narratives did they use? Did they refer to a traumatic moment of their lives? Can we speak of individual resilience or of a collective denial of their particular history? How did they react to the idea of displacement? Indeed, in the present series of interviews and their corresponding methodology, the subjectivity of our informants lies as the centre of an evolving story with different outcomes.²

Research and Methodology

From the vast array of Sephardim living in Montreal, we collected data of individuals belonging to different ethno-national groups to carefully explore the social memories of trauma and displacement through their individual experience. Aimed at collecting memories from mass violence, the oral history interviews follow the life story methodologies. The interviewees and interviewers explore the migrants' social world embedded in the narration of stories of the interviewees' new adopted country.

Within this framework, it is easier to question the aspects of the interviewees' migration within a post-Shoah, post-colonial context. Indeed, the Sephardi migrants' status as a religious minority in their home countries becomes a point of departure of the inquiry. We thus explored the possibilities and histories of *Sephardic Jews*, the name we gave to our subgroup within the group working on the "Holocaust and other persecutions against Jews."

The life stories were collected amongst Jews who were born in Arab-Muslim countries and settled in Montreal.³ We conducted 34 interviews, consisting of 14 women and 20 men. The average age of the interviewees was 70. The majority (21) came from Morocco, six came from Egypt, three from Lebanon, two from Iraq, and one from Algeria. Could the conditions for massive Sephardic migrations from Arab-Muslim countries be associated with human rights violations or with (coerced or not) displacements? These questions would form the

---

² The oral history method often involves a discrepancy between oral sources and interpretations by social sciences of the same events. Interviews are shaped by various factors, such as the individual being interviewed, the moment of the interview in time, as well as the direction given by the interviewer. The subjectivity and narrative forms of these sources allow us to analyze these testimonies within their "orality." The narratives are dependent on the perception of the individual and the boundary between external events involving the group and the subjectivity of the individual's perception.

³ We conducted these interviews with no time constraints or other restrictions. The interviewee was free to omit anything from the interview and, in fact, to terminate the interview at any moment. We located the interviewees through various social networks (friends, family, synagogue, holiday services, and word of mouth).

core of the present inquiry. Included in neither North African nor Middle Eastern history, the history of Sephardic/Oriental Jews raises a whole new set of substantive questions based on their departure from those countries in the mid-twentieth century (Gottreich and Schroeter 2011; Abécassis and Faü 2011).

Departure in a Post-Colonial Context

The departure of most Jews from these lands occurred suddenly and *en masse*. In the three decades following the Second World War, almost all Jews from *Maghreb* (North Africa) and *Machrek* (Middle East) left the countries where they had been living for centuries (Stillman 1979; Laskier 1994; Trigano 2009). The question remains as to how this displacement occurred and how the individual and collective stories of displacement contribute to the construction of a new set of narratives of Sephardic Jews settled in Montreal (Cohen 2010d) and of a Sephardic diaspora (Mays 2012).[4]

Montreal is characterized by the presence of a vocal minority of Jews who migrated during the sixties and seventies from North Africa and the Middle East. Their presence provided the incentive to further our understanding of their specific trajectories (Lasry and Tapia 1989; Berdugo-Cohen, Cohen, and Lévy 1987; Cohen and Guerry 2011). Furthermore, Montreal offers the ideal *neutral* space to analyze this group, a *third* place remote from the initial settings of both colonizer and colonized.

The history of the migration of Jews from the Arab-Muslim world has been at the centre of academic debate (Tsur 2001; Tsur 2007; Bin-Nun 2004; Shenhav 2007). Adopting a global perspective, Shmuel Trigano (2009) distinguishes between countries where Jews were "excluded" (such as Morocco) and countries where they were "expelled" (such as Algeria, Egypt, Syria, and Iran). Whereas Sami Chetrit (2004) considers the migration of North African Jews as a massive population displacement organized by Israeli Zionist organizations, Weinstock (2007) understand these departures against the backdrop of the ongoing humiliation attached to their status as *dhimmi*: that is, an ethno-religious minority recognized as a legitimate religious

---

[4] We will use here the term *Sephardi* when we are talking about the Sephardic community in Montreal, as it is a generic term that was chosen by those Jews who arrived from Arab-Muslim countries.

community but one subordinated to the Muslim majority under Islamic Law.

Coerced or not, the departure of Jews from the Maghreb-Machrek occurred in a context of violence different from one country to another. The displacement of Jews from Egypt is especially striking (Tolédano-Attias 2009). Of the 50,000 Jews living in Egypt before the Second World War, 40,000 left the country in 1956 and 1957, and another 5,000 had departed by 1967. Many factors were at play in the disappearance of Egypt's Jewish community, and the stories collected outline the importance of the question of denaturalization. Jews' legal status moved in this direction as new laws were applied to Jews between 1950 and 1956, provoking their massive departure from Egypt. Those who did not hold dual citizenship with another country became stateless. But furthermore, the migration of Maghrebi Jews took place after the violence of colonization and during the process of decolonization. Of course, it did not concern only the Jewish population, but colonization by France in the nineteenth century, and in the case of Morocco from 1912, came as a shock and was made possible by colonial wars (Rivet 2002). Violence during decolonization is exemplified by the war in Algeria but political uncertainty in Morocco (with a first coup attempt in 1971, for example) provided a feeling of insecurity. Beyond the mere situation of Jews, which is generally put in perspective in the interviews, one must consider the general context of colonial and post-colonial violence, within which their departure occurred.

Thus, we aim to analyze how Jews recollected their departure from Arab-Muslim lands, as this question is still fuelled by political and memorial issues (Cohen 2011). The use of oral history will allow us to better understand the relationship between memory and the trauma experienced with their departures. It raises the question of the categories used to define their migration and the violence stressed or undermined enshrined in their memories. Beyond testimony and trauma, we found collective and individual resilience: The interviewees recollect their subsequent migration and foster a reinterpretation of the past, both collectively and individually. The active memory of the Sephardic community has, since the migrants' arrival in Montreal, undergone a social transformation to allow them to adhere better to their new environment (Bédard 2007).

Analysis of the Interviews

Reactions to the theme of the interview brought an interesting dialogue right from the start. The use of the terms *persecution* together with *Holocaust* came as a shock to most of the people whom we wished to interview. Almost all our interviewees insisted on elucidating the title of our inquiry in the first contact: "Why are we talking about genocide? That's not us," or "We are not refugees, we paid for our own fare to come to Montreal," were among the first answers we received. Reticence to participate in the project, to reveal names, and to share certain stories was observed in both the pre-interviews and the interviews. The reaction of interviewees varied according to their native country, but their emotions and fearful reactions played on a spectrum of discomfort that remained lost in a collective silence. Perhaps, we thought, our interviewees did not see themselves as having been expelled or excluded from their own countries? But their emotional reactions and fear indicated otherwise. Our straightforward approach uncovered a whole new set of previously undisclosed feelings about their departures.

In the midst of a extensive displacement, where almost the totality of a group migrates, many individuals—but not the collectivity—might frame their departure within a forced or imposed setting (Akhtar 1999). This, of course, depends on many factors, including historical context, individual stories, collective perceptions, and shared memories. Within many narratives of the Sephardic community, a stoic bearing of difficult departure is perceived as a powerful force sustaining continuity and coherence. This process is exemplified in some of the life stories we share. The ability to be an agent rather than a victim of events legitimizes departure as a collectivity. This narrative enables departees to construct and reconstruct their history, and to show themselves as adaptable and malleable. However, on the other hand it undermines certain emotions that have been collectively ignored or marginalized and that remain conflicted within individuals' inner lives. The excavation of these emotions, including frustration and residual fear, could allow reconciliation between the individual's past and the group's history.

Comparing the migrations from Machrek and those from Maghreb sheds light on two types of displacement. In the first case, as noted, departure is perceived as an expulsion. Strong emotions are still present in recollections of the events. Fear and angst within the narratives reveal a possible sense of insecurity of the present, as well as a continuation of anger that could affect a possible reconciliation with their own past. Hence, it becomes essential to try to identify the factors of denial or forgetting. This aspect is a central element in certain interviews we collected, and some of the interviewees who came from Machrek, particularly those from Egypt or from Iraq, emphasized the forced dimension of their departure.

In the second case, that of the Maghreb, interviewees refused to consider their departure as expulsion. During the pre-interviews, Moroccan interviewees were particularly reluctant to assent to the terminology of the project. They did not consider themselves as displaced "by war" or by "other violations of their rights." Some professed that their departure stemmed from their own will or was linked to another aspect (familial or professional) that had no relation to any form of coercion. Indeed, the situation of Jews in Morocco was entirely different than that of Jews in Egypt. Moroccan independence in 1956 did not lead to discriminatory measures concerning Jewish-Moroccan nationality (Rivet 2002). Nevertheless, triggered by a feeling of insecurity, well-documented now by historians (Abitbol 2012), their departure took place over four decades, beginning with a mass migration to Israel in 1948, and continuing through the 1970s and 1980s, when the last contingents arrived in Canada. Their stories tend to emphasize the interviewees' freedom to choose their destination, sometimes downplaying the violence of the environment. In this sense, the plurality of migratory trajectories is quite significant. Furthermore, because these patterns are perceived and presented as "natural," we wanted to find out more about the administrative procedures undertaken to migrate. Thus, we discovered that the interviewees did not remember the administrative process involved in coming to Canada, or when they did, it was in a positive light. They associated this process with an ease seldom associated with the bureaucracy of immigration, thus downplaying the fear present in some of their narratives. Analyzing this lack of memory will help us understand how events are shaped and lived by individuals before becoming historical facts. We will look into the dichotomy between these different narratives.

Trauma and Stories of Forced Migrations

A first category of subjects stressed the forced dimension of their departure. How were these departures represented in their narratives?

Do these subjects consider themselves to be victims? In some cases, they refuse victimization. In these, what were the elements that allowed them to refuse to be defined as victims? The consequences of forced departures have been analyzed in many studies (Akhtar 1999), which emphasize that such forced departure tends to hurt individual development, accentuate the loss of national identity and citizenship, and thus provoke an internal schism, especially if expulsion occurred before adulthood.

The interview process allowed our subjects to construct and reconstruct their history, but it stirred up emotions that had been ignored collectively. Emotions such as fear, anger, and sadness often emerged in our interviews with people who had been forced to leave their country (essentially in Machrek) in a coercive manner. The issue of fear was present in some cases even before the interviews began. For instance, some interviewees chose to remain anonymous.[5] While not all participants who opted for anonymity did so due to fear, in some cases, fear was a factor. One person, for example, thought that revealing their name might cause retaliation on the part of the Moroccan government, expressing concern that if the interview fell into the hands of the "Moroccan police," they would be denied entry back into Morocco.

This aspect was especially prevalent in the case of Gérard, who was interviewed in 2011.[6] He was born in Egypt and left for France in 1956 after being expelled. He was a friend of one of the interviewer's parents and agreed to receive us for an interview. But he refused to sign the consent form, even with an anonymous status. The location of the project within Concordia University increased his doubts. The presence of a strong pro-Palestinian movement at this university, as well as the events of 2002, during which the Israeli Prime Minister Benjamin Netanyahu cancelled a speech he was invited to deliver on the campus after a hostile demonstration, raised the fear that these

---

[5] According to the ethics procedures of the Montreal Life Story Project, each participant could decide that their interview be transcribed—with the video and audio material destroyed—and all elements enabling knowledge of their identity erased. Nevertheless, people who chose this option had to sign a paper attesting to their acceptance of the project.

[6] Gérard did not accept to participate fully in the project and refused to sign the consent form. Nevertheless, he accepted to tell his story given the interviewee's word that he would remain anonymous. He was born in Alexandria in 1946 and he left Egypt for France in 1956. He then moved to Montreal.

interviews might "fall in the wrong hands." However, although Gérard did not trust the university, he was willing to share his story because he trusted the interviewers. Several other interviewees expressed the same misgivings.

Gérard's reluctance to participate in the project underlined the way he connected his past to present preoccupations concerning the situation in the Middle East. This case raised interesting questions about oral history and the attitude of interviewers. What can they do in situations in which procedures meant to protect interviewees were not sufficient in overcoming their apprehension when compared with other working groups? (High 2015).[7] The number of anonymous people in our group is very high—almost half of the group (6 out of 13), even though we conducted less than one-tenth of the interviews (34 out of 472).

Stories of interviewees who left their countries under duress were also imbued with anger and sadness. Egyptian Jews expelled in 1956 often recounted their departure with detail and precision. Maryse was born in Cairo and left Egypt with her family in 1956.[8] During the interview, she remembered very clearly when her parents were told that they had to leave. She recalled the "knocks on the door" that she heard before the officials entered the apartment. Gérard, as well, offered a very detailed description of his last day in Egypt.

Robert was born in Alexandria, in post-war Egypt.[9] He describes his departure as "a somewhat bitter pill for an exodus from Egypt, Exodus Two as they say, the second exodus, extremely painful and distressing." Here he reconfigures the traditional image of the Exodus,

---

[7] In total, 472 people were interviewed in multi-session interviews conducted in French (202), English (187), Khmer (49), Kinyarwanda (19), Spanish (14), and Arabic (1). Only 78 interviewees chose to place any restrictions on their interviews, with 65 limiting access (accessible only in archives, and a pseudonym must be used in quoting from the materials) and 13 opting for full anonymity.

[8] The interviews were part of the Life Stories of Montrealers Displaced by War, Genocide and Other Human Rights Violations project. Rules of ethics that the interviewers applied were those adopted by the project. The interviews were semi-structured and were, in most cases, conducted by two interviewers. According to the confidentiality rules of the project, we chose pseudonyms for interviewees who did not want to have their name published. Maryse was born in Cairo (Egypt) in 1948. Interview with Sara Cohen Fournier/Martin Messika, Montreal, 2012.

[9] Robert was born in 1946 in Alexandria. He moved to Cairo before leaving for France. Interview with Sara Cohen Fournier, Montreal, 2011.

celebrated during Passover, to encompass his own experience. Robert left Egypt when he was 17 years old under such violent circumstances that he cannot forgive his native country, even 50 years later. His father died a few years preceding the family's departure, a departure that was precipitated by the necessity of getting treatment for his mother's cancer that was only available in France. But when his family requested permission from the government to leave, they had to wait an entire year for their papers. Robert's recollection of the situation is vivid:

> When we arrived at Cairo airport to leave, my mother had colon cancer, was suffering greatly, in a wheelchair, receiving three injections of morphine per day to control the pain. Well, these barbarians in costumes imposed a complete physical search, and I will not go into details. I heard her scream in pain as they made the search to verify if she hadn't hidden jewels in her body. This went against the idea of Egypt as a tolerant country. To persecute a widow afflicted with cancer.

His enduring memories were supplemented by 50 years of retrospection. Robert detailed his own examination at the airport: "I, myself, was searched in a similar way, as well as my sister too […] so vexatious to the end." He started listing on his fingers: "They withdraw your citizenship, they give you a few dollars, and when you leave, they brand you with this indelible memory of molestation with this search for jewellery and money." Showing his ring, he continued: "All they left me with was my Bar Mitzvah ring and that's it […] And bye-bye! We left with a deep disgust for the country where we had lived for centuries and where even our ancestors had been happy for a period."

He considered this treatment an offence, to him and his family, perpetuating as it did the state of disgrace the Jews were put in, considered thieves of national property, spies working for Israel, or communists. Speaking of the departure of Jews from Egypt he said, "It was a beautiful system, well developed to get rid of its Jewish community and cause a maximum of damage without killing or assaulting people." He drew a parallel between his humiliating rejection by his former country and the loss of his mother, who died a year after their arrival in Paris.

These recollections developed into an obsession. His story is entrenched in memories that he deems "indelible." The Bar Mitzvah ring he wears daily symbolizes his lost youth, an object that links him to the past and crystallizes his sense of self within the context of unfinished forgiving. Robert often mentioned his inability to make peace with his native country—in a sense, cherishing these difficult emotions as part of his identity. "I do not have fond memories of my homeland and I hate to say that I am 'Egyptian,'" he told us, miming the quotation marks with his hands as he said *Egyptian*. "I say that I am a Jew from Egypt, and that's all. I have not made peace with this country because this country has never apologized for what they did, what they did to my family. I do not intend to forget these abuses."

Upon being forced out of Egypt, he was put in a liminal state. He was also frustrated by the non-responsiveness of international caring associations such as the Red Cross. In France, he was treated as a refugee. In the interview, he reaffirmed that "there will be no peace until there is recognition from the Egyptian government of what happened, but I'm sure I will never see that day." As was often the case in the interviews, the Israeli-Palestinian conflict also was present in his testimony. After describing his departure, he stated, "And we ended up […] the image on the other side of the problem of Palestinian refugees. Except that we picked up the pieces, restored our life and we tried to pursue a decent life without going to plant bombs left and right and kill people. So this is the story of Jews from Egypt."

Robert seemed to be looking for a sense of closure, a way for his past to be past and not remain a cloud hovering over him. Indeed, he stated during the interview, "[T]he emotions are still here." And later, he said, "[W]e must have been guilty somewhere for the simple fact of being Jewish at fifteen, sixteen." He did not feel capable of inserting the story of his departure within a broader perspective; indeed, he was still blaming himself. In effect, he had replaced other possible perspectives with anger and a complete rupture with his native country. He still hoped for some reconciliation, whereby the story of his stoically endured expulsion would be included in a more all-embracing, collective narrative. However, until this seriously took place, he continued to lack any personal and collective closure on his past.

Violence of the departure shaped a discourse of trauma that was captured in the interviews we conducted. In a post-Shoah era, where the experience of European Jews became the universal standard for collective trauma (Tint 2010), the space for Jews from Arab-Muslim countries to express their stories was relegated to the background. Indeed, their mass exodus was not associated with comparable massacres. Thus, the victims of these events are compelled to stay silent or advocate for themselves the position of "active players" in the collective memory. This was essentially the case for our interviewees who were coerced into leaving Egypt and Iraq.

From *Natural* Departures to Plural Trajectories

Discourses are plural and are linked to circumstances. Other interviewees, mostly those who came from Morocco, emphasized another dimension of the departing experience, which was not felt as a brutal rupture from their past lives. Rather, it seemed embedded in hazier memory, in which migrants adopted a diversity of migratory paths. In these interviews, narratives were built on the decision to leave, and they were imbued with silence and reticence.

In many cases, narratives of departures of people from Maghrebi origins were intertwined closely with work, study, or family necessities. These departures were considered by departees as a "natural," neutral move. It appeared as if there were no particular alarming causes for their departure, or at least such events and critical causes were obliterated from their memory and thus their narratives.

Arieh is an example of such migratory circulation: He left Casablanca, Morocco, for Israel in 1969, when he was 19 years old.[10] He arrived in Paris in 1972 and travelled in Europe before leaving for Montreal in 1974. Although he explained that he left for Israel because of his commitment to Zionism, he did not go into detail about his migratory experience. He indicated that after being in the Israeli army, "I turned [*j'ai tourné*], I ended up in England, and from there I went to Paris." He continued, "I was exploring, I did not know where I was going, I was a bit of a hippie." Going "on the road" at that time was not exceptional. In the 1960s, travelling after a stint in the army was common for young Israelis. However, Arieh's many trips must be put into perspective. He considered his departure from Morocco as difficult because he had to leave his family behind. However, he had nothing to say about leaving the country itself. Arieh provided few details on his state of mind at the time he left Morocco.

This vagueness and the reticence (Layman 2009) to develop the details that led to the departure were common among Moroccan

---

[10] Arieh was born in 1950 in Casablanca. He decided to leave for Israel with a group of young students in 1969. In 1972, he arrived in Paris where he had different jobs. He arrived in Montreal in 1974. Interview with Martin Messika/Ruxandra Petrinca, Montreal, November 2012.

interviewees. Through their willingness to "limit dialogue on specific matters" (Layman 210) interviewees exercise their authority and shape their narrative. Sometimes the boundaries between reticence and silence are not very clear. When we asked Arieh if he thought at the time he left that he would perhaps return to Morocco, he only answered, "No, I knew where I was going, even though I was very young, I did not want...no, I was not quite into it [*ça me disait rien*]." And in fact, he did not return to Morocco and settled finally in Montreal.

For us, the fact that the interviewees did not want to develop the reasons that led them to leave was a challenge, but it appears to be part of the narrative. As interviewers we had to carry out a "deep listening" (Sheftel and Zembrzycki 2010) in order to go further in this narrative without "plot." Thus, the complex trajectories (Israel, France, Canada, and the United States) were told in a way that considered the migration as *normal*. Interviewees seemed to be in survival mode. The relationships they had with other members of their families were relegated to a secondary role and seemed unimportant, not worth recalling. They did not even tell us if they discussed their decisions to leave with their families. Thus, getting information on their decisions to leave was difficult, and the overall impression was of a quick departure, with no one really in charge of taking care of the details of the destination of the family migration.

Pierre, born in Casablanca in 1928, held a managerial position in a bank.[11] In April 1957, he left during the first wave of Moroccan migration to Canada. According to his narrative, he decided to leave Morocco when bank employees went on strike. He recalls an incident that triggered his decision to leave, telling the story of how he ran into his "Muslim best friend" on the way to his office and the conversation they had:

> —Pierre, are you not going on strike?
> —You know well that I have responsibilities.
> —Well, if you are not afraid for your life, you should be for your daughter's. [...] I said "Okay, thanks." I left, and I headed directly [to plan my immigration].

---

[11] Pierre was born in 1928 in Casablanca. He left Morocco for Canada in April 1957, with his wife and child. He first arrived in Toronto but left soon after for Montreal. He found employment in a bank. Interview with Martin Messika, Montreal, November 2011.

Pierre never felt any affiliation with the strikers. He considered his position to be a higher one, where one does not go on strike but rather works. He understood a conversation with a "Muslim" colleague as a disguised threat against him and his family. Already feeling displaced in his workplace, and while his words meant that he was reacting as a manager, he interpreted the situation, rightfully or not, as an ethno-religious conflict ("I am threatened as a Jew, so I should leave, now"). However, he did not elaborate on the various aspects of the situation, and a little while later in the interview, he presented his decision to leave in different terms: "I did not leave because I was scared; I left because I did not like to be told [...] well [...] I do not like what is mandatory." Pierre did not stress the verbal violence of his friend's expressions, nor did he express his own emotions. He perhaps underestimated the danger of the conflict in which he nevertheless felt trapped. Rather, Pierre preferred to assert his autonomy. According to him, he was not forced to leave but decided that he *had* to go. Leaving was not linked to a feeling, but to the application of a principle ("I do not like what is mandatory"). Violence, feelings, and fear were not the primary points of emphasis in his interview; on the contrary, he insisted on his ability to make a rational decision to leave, which he did without a second thought.

This "general atmosphere," in which Jews felt unwanted, induced our interviewees to leave Morocco. Paradoxically, if the decision could be taken quickly, almost on the spur of the moment, bringing the immigration project to fruition could prove difficult. However, amid the fierce political battles conducted by international Jewish organizations to "save the Jewish community of Morocco," many felt that they had to leave (Bin-Nun 2004). In the interviews, these experiences led the interviewees to undermine certain aspects, which was a challenge for us as interviewers. Analyzing the concrete, administrative steps that had to be taken to migrate to Canada can help us understand better the nature of their departure.

The *Ease* of Immigrating to Canada

Interviewees from Morocco emphasized neither being treated with violence nor the forced dimension of their departure. Subjects tended to consider migration as a rational decision. At different points, interviewees stressed the fact that leaving was the result of their own decision and that they were not forced to leave, though at the same time they referred to violent events. But *planning to leave* and the act of *leaving* are very different steps, especially considering the material difficulty involved in getting a visa or a passport.

Interviews with Jews from Morocco would have us believe that getting to Canada was easy. This dimension was seldom present in their stories, since the interviewees who left with their parents were not in charge of planning this departure. But how did it work for the adults? Viviane, who was married and had a child, arrived in Montreal in 1965.[12] She did not have a strong memory of the procedures her family had to go through to arrive in Canada: "My husband oversaw it. It was not very difficult, even if it was a bit long, one year or two, but it was not very difficult.… I do not remember it as a handicap."

Other interviewees mentioned the names of two agencies: the Jewish Immigrant Aid Services (JIAS) and Hebrew Immigrant Aid Society (HIAS). In their memories, these two associations were often confused. Whereas JIAS was a Canadian, Montreal-based, immigration agency, United-HIAS-Service was a US Jewish organization that worked in Europe and in Morocco. They worked together, but the interviewees were not interested in their specific fields of activity.

Pierre was proud to tell us that he knew a HIAS agent, S. Plasterek, who worked in Casablanca, in charge of immigration procedures. His account was more precise than Viviane's but remained ambiguous. The ease with which he obtained his immigration papers was surprising. After his altercation with his Muslim friend at the bank he

> went directly to JIAS [sic].… I told Mr. Plasterek, "I'm going to the United States." Mr. Plasterek answered: "You are going to wait a long time to go to the United States. Why don't you go to the anteroom of the United States, to Canada? With your skills, you will be able to enter immediately." I said "go on" [*allez-y*]. Very soon after, he got me a visa.

The vagueness of these descriptions is quite striking. There is no mention of the many forms people had to gather to prepare their visa, nor of the role of Canadian immigration officials in this procedure and these descriptions evoke the image of immigration to Canada as being

---

[12] Viviane was born in 1942 in Casablanca into a family of three girls and three boys. She left Casablanca with her husband and her child in 1963. Interview with Martin Messika/Claudia Itzkowich, Montreal, November 2012.

easy, a mere formality. Administrative procedures were imbued with a *magic* dimension.

Jewish organizations were instrumental in enabling Jews from Morocco to come to Canada. But what they saw as a mere formality made by one person (the HIAS agent in Casablanca), was in reality a project that involved a transnational coalition of associations lobbying the Canadian government to include Jews from Morocco in a special category of immigrants. Our interviewees do not remember being in contact with a Canadian immigration official, but the contact existed between them and Jewish agencies. The *ease* enshrined in their discourse does not mean that immigrating to Canada was easy, but rather that all the administrative/bureaucratic process, both in Morocco and in Canada, was dealt with in its entirety by these agencies. The project implied strong networking within the state's agencies and staff, as well as the ability to work discreetly.

Here again, the victimization of the Jews, seen as a vulnerable population, which prompted their rescue by international Jewish organizations, was absent from our informant's stories. Interviews conducted with Jews from Morocco did not detail the procedures of immigration. If the issue of *papers* arose, it was generally in connection with the Moroccan administration. Little was said about Canadian officials since the Jewish agencies were the main contacts for prospective Moroccan immigrants.

Beyond this example of immigration procedure, the discrepancy between the accounts we get from oral history interviews and the accounts we get from other historical sources is patent. Quite striking is the undervaluation of the role of Jewish organizations in this process. At some point, subjects were willing to stress the fact that they chose to go to Canada and did not link their departure with the proactive action of North American-Jewish immigration agencies.

In the policies they carried out concerning North African Jewry, Jewish international organizations were concerned with the danger these populations faced were they to remain in their respective countries while Israel was at war (Bin-Nun 2004). At the basis of the deal between Jewish-Canadian organizations and the federal government was the idea that North African and Moroccan Jewry were in danger and had to be *saved* by leaving for Canada. For the interviewees, their refusal to recognize the action of Canadian-Jewish organizations (thus minimizing their debt to the mainly Ashkenazi-Jewish establishment) in the immigration process conveyed the idea that they were not in need of saving, as they were not in danger. The *magic* process of getting a visa to Canada enabled them to refuse victimhood and emphasized the freedom they possessed to choose their destination.

Stories of departure of Jews from Maghreb and Machrek enshrined memories from their lives in a post-colonial context as well as contemporary preoccupations and fears. Departures shaped the way interviewees remembered ethnic and religious conflicts in their country of birth. Some of them had a very precise memory of a violent event, while others remembered "small events," everyday life conflicts, which bear a particular value in the memory of migration and brought them to feel that no future was possible in their homelands.

The cases shared in this chapter stress different departure experiences of Jews from Arab-Muslim countries. Within the diversity of national contexts, these stories provide an idea of the process by which the issue of victimhood is reformulated. We saw that strong emotions emphasized the forced dimension of the migration, while other interviewees put in perspective the plurality of their migratory trajectory and show reticence in going into details. We can also say that the *magic* and *effortlessness* of their departure are linked to the desire not to be assimilated as a victim, and to be able to understand their trajectory as a choice rather than an imposition or a given possibility. Either facing deep political turmoil or the collective eagerness to leave, individuals from different national backgrounds reasserted their trajectories in strong, autonomous ways.

Furthermore, by comparing these stories with information derived from other sources, we can see how memory selects elements and participates in the building of a collective memorial. These memories help the collectivity forget the (traumatic) past and give individuals the adaptability and agility to get up and go when the situation becomes tense. This continuity reflects the biblical comprehension of the Exodus, where the narrative offers not a comprehensive, sequential narrative, but rather an episodic account of the different moments of the migration (Sarna 1989). Hence, by leaving some aspects of their departure behind, they attempt to build up memories from a specific collective identity, which in turn contributes to the construction of this new diaspora's identity. The resistance displayed by some individuals in confronting the traumatic events in their lives reveals how much their identity is still one of survival and dislocation.

Our research on Jews from Arab-Muslim lands in Montreal revealed a comprehensive picture of their departures. Whether as the result of difficult political situations or through the invisible help of Jewish agencies, the stories collected are interwoven by this heritage of adaptation to new situations through departure and the ability of those individuals to reconstitute a collective identity in a diaspora. Through identifying with the ancient Sephardic diaspora, they connect themselves to a rich and venerable history of high culture and transnational networks.

Finally, the conflicting memories between voluntary or forced displacements of Jewish populations from the Maghreb-Machrek, although largely connected to the specifics of national histories, are embedded in a larger conflict between the religious majority (Arab Muslims) and the minority (Jews), which came to a head with the Israeli-Palestinian conflict. The post-Shoah and post-colonial contexts have raised this issue to its most extreme level: Jews as the ultimate victim. Paradoxically, during much of the five decades since their first departure from Arab-Muslim countries, our interviewees desired to erase this history and its image of victimization to replace it with a plurality of stories, more typical of post-colonial, free-floating migrations. Others keep their stories to themselves, waiting for their former nation's recognition of what happened. In either case, interviewees do not compare themselves with Shoah survivors. Therefore, as it is also difficult for them to consider themselves as victims, their own stories fit better into a diaspora narrative of the post-colonial type, one of continuous migration. In effect, the departures of Maghreb Jews preceded the mass migration of Maghreb Muslims in the 1970s and onward, including to Canada, from 2000 until the present time.

CHAPTER 6

Forgetting and Forging: My Canadian Experience as a Moroccan Jew

Yolande Cohen

Like most teenagers, I dreamed of a freedom from all the hurdles and family obligations (Cohen 2020a). It was the 1960s and I was then living in Meknès, Morocco, a city where I felt I had no place. Immersed at school and with my friends in the mainly English music and film subculture, I longed to live elsewhere, maybe in America. My American fantasy seemed unreal: too far, too complicated. But I still had a strong desire to escape a tight and stifling atmosphere. I did not entirely belong to the Jewish community because I was not part of the *mellah*, as I was living in the French Ville Nouvelle and went to French schools; and I could not take part in the French colonial culture, since I was an *Israélite marocaine*, even though I spoke French *sans accent*. Nor, as a Jew, did I belong to the Muslim-Moroccan majority. Like many other Moroccans, I spoke enough *darija* (vernacular) Arabic but not classical Arabic, even though I took four years of Arabic classes in the French lycée I attended. Truly, I spoke only Judeo-Arabic, the language of my grandmother. And even though I had friends in each sector of this outpost of the French colonial empire, where the Alaouite had once constructed theirs, I felt estranged from all of them. Growing up in Meknès as a Jewish girl, I was caught in the maelstrom of the last decade of the French colony and the explosion of Moroccan independence. So, when I finished high school, after a year of accrued tensions with my family and at the high school, I decided to go to France to study at the university. I am still amazed that I was able to "convince" my parents of such a project.

How could an eighteen-year-old girl leave her family and hometown in the 1960s? I figured that I could finally be free from my family and from the community tensions that were overwhelming our daily lives. Those tensions became volatile with the Arab-Israeli wars and the exile of most of our Jewish neighbours and friends in the 1960s and 1970s. For the minority of Jews who stayed in Morocco then, the relation to Israel was complex: a dream for the promised land as well as a land overtaken by wars. We received little news from my father's family—his four brothers and three sisters and their many young children—who moved to Israel in September 1948. But my newlywed parents, who had already moved to Marseille to join them, knew that the war was raging and were reluctant to follow them. Instead, they came back to Meknès and raised their four children there. Still, we could not talk in public about Israel, since the Israeli-Palestinian wars had direct consequences on us living in Arab-Muslim lands. My own memories of Israel were contradictory: both present and absent. It was constantly there but had to be silenced. This feeling, it turned out, would be enduring, even in my life in Canada.

As soon as I could travel alone, at eighteen, I made my first visit to Paris and then to Israel. Even though I was not engaged in Zionist activities, I was drawn by the kibbutz life and all the socialist rhetoric I heard about it. I wanted to check in with many of my friends in high school who had been ardent Zionists and had made Aliyah in 1967. I stayed at a kibbutz in the Galilee, and even enrolled as a student at the Hebrew university in political science. But very quickly, after a few months of *Oulpan* (intensive Hebrew lessons), I had to leave. I was unable to make Israel my own country and went back to Paris to study. This does not mean I did not have the strongest ties to Israel. How could it be different when half of my family lived there? Yet, I felt that it was not for me.

A baby boomer, educated from grade 1 in the French schools, I thought of myself as mainly French. I did not really share my friends' idealism, since, unlike them, I was not a Zionist. I thought I belonged in Paris. In fact, I did not think I had any other choice, even though other friends went on to study in Casablanca or Rabat, which had public and tuition-free universities, or in Israel, if they were Zionists; but most of my peers at the French lycée went to France. For the brightest students of either nationality, and for all the French, France's universities seemed to be the only choice. For some Jewish girls who had family in France, it was also one of the best options. Eager to give me a good education but unable to stop me, my parents accepted my decision to leave. I promised to stay with family in Paris, but quickly found another place to live my student life.

In Paris it did not take long to discover that I was not French, but a Jewish girl of Moroccan nationality. Alongside all the other migrants seeking to get their official papers, I spent many hours at the Préfecture de police in Paris, year after year, to renew my papers. Nothing was more concrete than this bureaucratic experience to understand the colonial logic: It was a litmus test of its contradictions. How could it be that I had to ask for a visa to stay in Paris, when I was raised with the idea that France was my only homeland (*patrie*)? Feeling rather than knowing the effects of the colonization on the colonized, I thought this was utterly unfair. I thought maybe I should tell them that I was almost French and clear up the situation by seeking French naturalization. Twice I went through the naturalization process, filed naturalization forms, thinking that this would correct what I thought was just a mistake, a misunderstanding, a *malentendu*, as Camus put it. After all, the French in Morocco taught me how to speak and behave like a French girl; they certainly succeeded, and I felt like one of them! I kept wondering why my applications were rejected. Not long ago, years after the fact but with the emotions linked to this blunt rejection still vivid, I went to the archives to check the *reasons* given by the French officials for rejecting my naturalization applications. They turned out to be pretty obvious: I was a student, my parents were still living in Morocco and not in France, and I had no regular income. Like most Moroccans, I did not have special access to French citizenship. This fuelled my anger even more: against the French government, against the French colonial power, against the capitalist order.

May '68 in Paris

I joined the student movement that was booming in 1968. By then, the events of May–June 1968 were still unfolding in the universities. I joined a leftist group, which changed my life completely. I finally found a place where I could belong: A cosmopolitan and internationalist movement was the ideal way to convey my anger and transform it into political activism. It also provided the ideal space where I could forget who I was and forge a new identity as an active citizen of the world. As a history student, I started thinking that I might one day want to teach and use my skills to make a living and become a professional historian. If studying in Paris presented me with some administrative problems, it was nothing compared to finding a job in the profession I wanted.

Not being a French citizen, I could not prepare the *concours d'agrégation*, the key that opened the doors of teaching in the high school or university system in France. I sought the advice of my thesis supervisor, who was a communist and who later became the head of the Ligue des droits de l'Homme. All she said was that a Moroccan-Jewish girl like me could not pretend she could get a job as a teacher because such positions were reserved for nationals; even her own son could not get one! (And he was much more credentialed than I was!) My hard-won degrees could not translate into a career. It took me some time to realize the implications of this situation, and I almost dropped out from the university as I was finishing my dissertation, working all the while at minimum wage on the side. It was clear that I was not going to find a job in Paris, other than the odd ones that a cousin could provide in his business. And even though I was very active in the Trotskyist and feminist movements there, which really were filling my life, I could not envision staying there once my citizenship application was rejected.

At that point, my parents and siblings had finally decided, after much thought, to move from Meknès to Montreal. It was 1974. It crushed me to see that they were finally quitting our hometown, where almost none of our family and friends remained. But their decision was made. They would join my mother's family, already established in Montreal. I visited them the following summer, and—surprisingly—very much liked Montreal and the Laurentians, where my cousins and their friends had a chalet.

Moving to Montreal

Even though Quebec was not at all in my plans, the fact that my parents had moved there, and that I did not see any interesting future for me in Paris, led me to make the move a couple of years after them. It was pretty easy to get the visa as an immigrant in Canada compared with the hurdles I went through in France. As it happens, I got my doctorate degree, found a job at Université du Québec à Montréal, and have been teaching contemporary French history ever since. I remained attached to my friends in Paris and keep going back often. I go back to Morocco, too, as well as Israel, where I have a large family and a strong emotional attachment. Even though I still bear the stigma of an immigrant, traumatized by my family's quick departure from Morocco and by the hardship of multiple migrations, Montreal became the place where I found myself: I got married, raised two beautiful children, and pursued the career I dreamed of.

For me, there is no better place to be than Montreal! I became a Québécois and a Canadian, of Moroccan-Jewish origin. In a way, the possibility of keeping a multiplicity of belongings is perhaps the greatest factor that makes Canada a hospitable place for immigrants.

How does this personal narrative fit within the wider story of Moroccan-Jewish post-colonial migration? While there are as many narratives as there are immigrants, my personal trajectory fits well within the evidence-based history of Moroccan-Jewish migration in Quebec and, more broadly, in Canada. Overall, this group has fared quite well economically, and has been successful in settling in Canada, compared with other groups who arrived at the same time, such as the Haitians or the Chileans. Two main factors account for this success. On the one hand, the new immigrants were quite young and educated. On the other, their integration was facilitated by a vast mobilization of Montreal's Jewish institutions and their professional social workers.

Their actions not only were crucial to help open the Canadian borders to non-Europeans, but they also helped find jobs and housing for new migrants and afforded them opportunities to socialize, initially inside the mainly Ashkenazi community, first in Montreal and then in Toronto. Maybe the feeling of being too much indebted to the established community led some of them to worry about how they could give it back. A fierce people with strong community traditions, Moroccan Jews resented the humiliating position they were in. Many of them who told our research team (Cohen 2017; Cohen, Messika, and Cohen Fournier 2015; Cohen 2014b) their story of migration had *forgotten* the help given to them by JIAS: They did not remember the migration process as being a hard one, nor did they recall being helped to arrive in Montreal. Forgetting the hardship of immigration is one sure way to hide or deny the trauma of leaving one's country. The problem is that it becomes complicated to relate to your own story and to make sense of it. In my view, this is what happened with the changes that followed in their/our own representation.

Stories of Moroccan Jews in Canada: Becoming Sephardi Jews

For the last 35 years I have been doing fieldwork in a community I belong to, alternating between sharing its fate (my personal emotions) and keeping a necessary distance (the scholar's gaze). I would like to outline some of the complicated accommodations that have been going on since I arrived in Canada.

I found that most of this population had clung to its long-held tradition of maintaining its own community organizations. In Morocco, it was meant to preserve its identity as a Jewish minority; in Quebec it was a way of preserving its Moroccan Jewishness. We can see this influence in two very important institutions Moroccan Jews created as soon as they arrived: their own synagogues and schools. Even if most of these migrants were secular Jews, the few young men, with some women, who founded the Association francophone des juifs nord-africains, which became the Communauté sépharade du Québec (CSQ), wanted to establish themselves as an autonomous group, but not a religious one. Their model was the Conseil des communautés israélites du Maroc, which functioned as a federation of local communities, electing a board approved by the king. The rabbis, although relatively autonomous, were nominated by the community, and the nomination of the head rabbi was also to be approved by the king. The rabbis chosen to compose the judiciary (*Tribunal rabbinique*) for all civil questions are officials paid by the Ministry of Justice. It is interesting to note that in a monarchy, where state and religion are not separated, all matters of religion are clearly delineated to fit the status of each religious group.

We could see that this model was brought to Quebec by those who built the structure of the CSQ, only this model does not quite fit within the Montreal-Jewish community. So, when they decided to bring a rabbi from Morocco (Rabbi Sabbah) to perform what they thought could be the Sephardi Chief Rabbi, they were opposed by the Vaad (the Montreal Rabbinate) and faced the difficult task of delineating its field of competence within the CSQ. It did not take long to see the arrangement fail, mostly due to infighting but also to the different organization of the Jewish communities in Quebec. So instead of having one chief rabbi, Moroccan Jews had several rabbis who officiated at the many synagogues they founded in Montreal and Toronto. If in Canada the state is secular, unlike in Morocco, Judaism can be practised without any established authority, with the result that there is a plural market for "Moroccan Judaism" here that the immigrants themselves never knew back home. It was therefore not very difficult for Moroccan Jews to continue to practise their religious rituals the way they wanted. The large number of synagogues and religious centres devoted to Sephardi or Jewish-Moroccan cults and traditions in Montreal and Toronto attest to that.

As far as the schools were concerned, the strong influence of the Alliance israélite universelle, established in Morocco with its mixed school system, is obvious. The creation of the École Maïmonide in Montreal by the CSQ as early as 1969 clearly indicates Moroccan Jews' will to assert their presence in separate institutions. In Toronto, they did not create such schools but integrated in the predominantly anglophone school system, whether Jewish or otherwise. But they created their own cultural centre (such as the Kehila Centre for instance) to transmit their Jewish-Moroccan traditions and rituals, as well as Hebrew lessons and religious education.

As most of the new Moroccan-Jewish immigrants spoke French at a time when French was becoming Quebec's predominant language, it was quite clear that this meant that Moroccan Jews diverged from Jewish immigrant patterns of integrating in the mainly anglophone group. Their determination to keep French as their main language and to establish themselves in French culture became their main asset in a time when Quebec was asserting the predominance of French in its laws (Bill 101, for example). The arrival of this group of immigrants gave birth to a separate entity based on a renewed Sephardic identity. It is difficult to know exactly how the decision to change the name of their Association des juifs nord-africains came about, but the consensus fell on the term *Sephardic* Jews, rather than Arab, Oriental (which would be the translation of Mizrahi), North African, or Maghrebi. Some members who came from formerly Spanish Morocco (Tangier, Melilla) found that Sephardic would be the appropriate name for them, since it meant retaining their old traditions from Spain. Some others wanted to gather the other Jews who were already present in Montreal—such as the Egyptians, the Iraqis, and others—under their umbrella.

The Spanish and Portuguese Synagogue, which attracted many Moroccan Jews on their arrival, was founded by Sephardic families 250 years ago. This particular combination of people and the overall landscape of the Jewish community in Montreal led some to identify with an ancient Sephardic world. For the anglophone leadership, which was very much aligned with Israel and cared much about its pro-Israel support, it was also an acceptable compromise. After many years of tensions and recriminations, exiles and departures to Toronto or elsewhere, it became obvious to all that a francophone segment of the Montreal-Jewish community could be an asset in Quebec. It is striking to note that while French Canadians were renewing their own identity as Québécois, Jews of Moroccan origins became Sephardi as well as Québécois.

After many years of difficult debates to get some public recognition for Moroccan Jews as a community, the question of asserting its own different identity ceased to be important after 11 September 2001. The harsh reality of a growing antisemitism, fuelled both by the populist and extreme right and by an expanding Islamist radicalism, changed their perception and the ways in which they could relate to the greater Jewish community. Religious radicalism, and Islamophobia in particular, and the pre-eminence of religion in the public sphere are now at the centre of the political realm. If in Canada the multicultural position has always encouraged the expression of individual and community (religious) identity, it is not so in Quebec, where a strong movement in favour of integral secularism (*laicity*) is prevalent. It was finally time for the Sephardi community to join with the rest of the Jewish community in reasserting their identity as Jews.

Commemoration of Canadian History: Jews as Settlers and Immigrants

Numerous celebrations marked the 150th anniversary of the foundation of the Canadian federation. The many groups composing the Canadian mosaic had different, often contradictory, views of why and how Canadians should remember this moment in particular, since many people could claim different dates to celebrate. For the First Nations, it was at best a non-event, since they were the founding nations, well before anybody claimed their lands. For others, including many in Quebec who resented the federation as an imposition of a colonial power on their own sovereign nation, there was nothing worth celebrating. If anything, this moment meant the subjection of a proud people (the Québécois) to what they perceived as a foreign power (the Anglo-Protestant Canadians).

For us Jews, who as a religious minority have long lived in the margins, if not excluded or discriminated against, we can seize this moment to think about our past and present relations to this history. I like to think that, as a member of the Spanish and Portuguese Synagogue, I am now connected to an ancient migration. Jewish migration and settlement in New France have made the Jewish contribution to Canadian history important and ancient. We are celebrating the 250th anniversary of the Spanish and Portuguese Synagogue, the second synagogue on the continent that was established by English settlers of Sephardi origins in Montreal. Those pioneers kept the name of their countries of origin, even though they were the descendants of the survivors of the 1492 Catholic Inquisition, which chased them from Spain and Portugal. The Hart and Joseph families named their congregation Shearith Israel, the Remnants of Israel now scattered in Canadian soil. Their contribution is hardly known, but mostly their ancient presence has contributed to the making of Canadian history.

The mention of Jewish officers and merchants in the British contingent arriving in Quebec in 1763 signals their participation in the colonial enterprise. This small Jewish group of Sephardi settlers who built the first institutions of the Montreal-Jewish community was part of the anglophone elite of Montreal. Rapidly overwhelmed by the arrival of large waves of Jewish immigration from the central European ghettos in the late nineteenth and early twentieth centuries, the Montreal-Jewish community was transformed into a plurality of ethnic groups who spoke both Yiddish and English. The rapid integration of this small Sephardic group in the Anglo-Protestant elite was quickly forgotten with the arrival of an important contingent of eastern European Jews. The Sephardi elite narrative of Canadian-Jewish history receded behind a new narrative focused on Ashkenazi non-elites. The backbone of this new Canadian-Jewish narrative has it that Jewish migrants, expelled and fleeing their old countries' antisemitism, built thriving communities and experienced first-hand, as ethnic groups, the pluralism of Canadian polity. Not only has the Sephardic content of this history disappeared but its settler's aspect has been replaced by a migrant one. So even if (Sephardi) Jews have settled in Canada for over 250 years, Jews' settlement in Canada became synonymous with twentieth-century Ashkenazi migrations.

As a relatively new migrant myself, I was happy to dig into this history to find those ancient Sephardic traces in Montreal, which make me part of an ongoing history, albeit very distant and different from my own. But I also keep on drawing comparisons between here and there, Montreal and Meknès, my hometown in Morocco, and between Paris, the city where I studied and got engaged with adult life, and Montreal, the city where I now live and work. I am happy to celebrate Jewish holidays with my family at the Spanish and Portuguese Synagogue. It gives me a sense of purpose to set my foot where other Sephardi Jews have been. For me, and perhaps for others like me, migrating to Canada was a dream come true. Here, I feel that I can renew my attachments to a larger Sephardi diaspora, rooted in a very ancient history and now dispersed all over the world.

A Sephardi Jewish Diaspora of the Modern Times, with Israel as Its Centre

Does this mean that there is a global Sephardi Jewry with a more or less unique way of seeing oneself, whether we live in Paris, Tel-Aviv, or Montreal? There are many ways to be part of a Jewish diaspora today, as there are many ways to be Sephardi. Living today in Montreal, Canada seems to me even better than my dream of going to the United States. If the attraction of the United States has been extraordinary for my generation in the 1960s and 1970s, not too many Moroccan Jews made it directly there. Instead, we came to Canada largely because of the organized migration led by JIAS.

I too share an attachment to religion, Israel, and the Holocaust, which are considered to be the three main pillars that define today's North American Jewry. My emotional attraction, one associated with expressing my identity, is a feeling of being different. When I was a child, I was taught that being Jewish meant having a strong family/community attachment, representing our alliance with God, and respecting some if not all the rituals, which in effect were differentiating us from everybody else around us. Did it mean I was religious? Not really. I considered myself a Jew in an Arab world, in which religion defined everyone's identities. My relation to the Holocaust and Israel is part of what we are today as Jews, forever part of my identity.

And I am quite aware that being a Jew and a Canadian citizen are all compatible with these ties to another country and other emotional attachments.

A plural society allows for such diverse loyalties. Canada is such a place.

CHAPTER 7

A Piece of a Torah Scroll in My Basement

Yolande Cohen

My parents Aaron Cohen and Marie Berdugo Cohen had to leave their town, Meknès, Morocco, in haste in the winter of 1974 (Cohen 2022). They felt the situation was dire enough for them and their three children to decide that it was finally time to leave their beloved country. After much debate and tears, and as their whole family had already left for Casablanca and then France and Canada, they opted to go to Montreal where my mother's sisters and nephews were already established.

Since their departure was planned a few months earlier, they had time to think of what they would bring with them to Montreal. A friend offered them space in a cargo container that was due to leave Casablanca for Montreal, so they started packing their stuff and delivered it to the port, one truck at a time. They chose the month of Ramadan, a fasting time, to move each parcel and piece of furniture quietly, during the three-hour period when their Muslim neighbours broke their fast at sunset, not to raise their suspicion. They did not wish to attract attention, even though everyone knew that the Jews had been leaving the city and the country *en masse*, over the preceding 20 years or so. It was difficult enough to leave everyone they knew, without greeting them or saying goodbye, so I guess they felt that they could not burden themselves even more. They had to leave without anyone noticing, hiding their exile from everyone.

So, the decision of what to take and what to leave had been weighted constantly during those few months preceding their departure. They certainly could not leave behind certain things, such as their sacred objects, essential pieces of their identity. But such objects cannot be transported easily because they are sacred. For the remaining members of the Jewish community, the question of what to do with those ancient and beautiful Sepharim as well as the many prayer books was a painful one. Once it was known that my parents were leaving, my father was tasked to take with him some of the Torah scrolls left behind in empty synagogues.

My father had already taken the very ancient Sepher Torah from his family synagogue, which could not be used anymore because it had been altered somehow, therefore unfit for a synagogue. So, he did not hesitate to take with him two more, as a mitzva. Those were newest and were to be relocated where they could be used. So, they brought with them to Montreal three Torah scrolls (Sepher Torah) from Meknès. When in Montreal, he had to dispose of them. One of them went to France, at his niece's demand to garner her husband's new synagogue in Montrouge; the other one went to Florida at one of his friend's requests.

He kept the most ancient one, which had been in his family for four generations. When we made a donation of a piece of the Torah scroll to the McCord Museum for the Shalom Montreal exhibition in 2018, he was interviewed to tell its story. He underlined how important it was for his family to have a Torah scroll handwritten by erudite scribes on original kosher sheep skin, with special ink that resisted through more than a century, and how he could not leave Morocco without it. Even if the Sepher Torah could not be used for ritual reading, since it was too old and scratched and therefore *asoul* or desecrated, he wanted to keep it in the family as a piece of archive. He did cut some pieces out to distribute to each of his children for their Bar Mitzvah, where the *Peracha* of the week was inscribed, and kept the rest of the scroll in paper, covered and revered as an ancient tribute to their life past. For my siblings, it became the sign or a witness to this ancient Jewish tradition of praying and reading the Torah and of the faith and dedication to Judaism of our grandparents and our great grandparents.

It travelled the oceans to reach Canada, where pieces of it are now on our walls, in nice settings celebrating an ancient craft, or laying in our cupboards, or at the museum. Now that my father has passed away, we are indebted to his decision to bring this incredible document with him to Montreal. For us and for the people who are watching over it, it is an archive that presents an ancient way of life, where Moroccan Jews expressed their faith through practical arrangements. Everything in this Torah scroll is modest though extraordinarily elaborate.

My next move is to give the rest of this Torah scroll to the Montreal Holocaust Museum, as a tribute to my family's exile.

Figure 7.1. A piece of a Torah scroll.
Source: Private collection of Yolande Cohen.

Bibliography

Articles and Books published by Yolande Cohen and others

Books

Cohen, Yolande, ed. 2000. *Juifs marocains à travers les âges. Tradition et modernité* (8 h). Cédérom Doxa Média.
Cohen, Yolande. 2010a. *Femmes philanthropes : catholiques, protestantes et juives dans les organisations caritatives au Québec.* Presses de l'Université de Montréal.
Cohen, Yolande, ed. 2017. *Les sépharades au Québec : parcours d'exils nord-africains.* Del Busso.
Cohen Yolande, Mireille Calle-Gruber, and Élodie Vignon. 2014. *Migrations maghrébines compares : genre, ethnicités et religions (France/Québec, de 1945 à nos jours).* Riveneuve.
Cohen, Yolande, and Joseph Lévy. 1992. *Itinéraires sépharades. 1492–1992 : mutations d'une identité.* Grancher.
Lasry, Jean-Claude, Joseph Lévy, and Yolande Cohen, eds. 2007. *Identités sépharades et modernité.* Presses Université de Laval.

Articles and Chapters

Cohen, Yolande. 2008. "Femmes, vie associative et politique : perspectives théoriques." In *Le Maroc aujourd'hui*, edited by Paola Gandolfi and Quaderni Merifor, 245–260. Venise: Casa Editrice Il Ponte.
Cohen, Yolande. 2010b. "Le genre d'une migration postcoloniale : de Meknès (Maroc) à Montréal (Québec)." *Genre et histoire* 6.
Cohen, Yolande. 2010c. "Juifs au Maroc, Séfarades au Canada. Migrations et processus de construction identitaire." *Archives juives* 2 (43): 132–144.
Cohen, Yolande. 2010d. "Migrations juives marocaines au Canada ou comment devient-on sépharade ?" In *Les communautés juives de Montréal. Histoire et enjeux contemporains,* edited by Pierre Anctil and Ira Robinson, 234–252. Québec: Septentrion.
Cohen, Yolande. 2011. "The Migrations of Moroccan Jews to Montreal: Memory, (Oral) History and Historical Narrative." *Journal of Modern Jewish Studies* 10 (2): 245–262.

Cohen, Yolande. 2013a. "Juifs du Maghreb au Canada." In *Canada's Jews. In Time, Space and Spirit*, edited by Ira Robinson, 168–183. Boston: Academic Studies Press.

Cohen, Yolande. 2013b. "Mémoires des migrations de juifs marocains à Montréal." In *Remembering War, Genocide and Other Human Rights Violations*, edited by Steven High, Edward Little, and Ry Duong, 250–276. Toronto: University of Toronto Press.

Cohen, Yolande. 2014a. "Les juifs sépharades à Montréal." In *Histoires d'immigration au Québec*, edited by Claude Corbo, Guy Berthiaume, and Sophie Montreuil, 95–110. Montreal: Les Presses de l'Université du Québec.

Cohen, Yolande. 2014b. "The Migrations of Moroccan Jews to Montréal: Memory, (Oral) History and Historical Narrative." In *Sites of Jewish Memory: Jews in and from Islamic Lands in Modern Times*, edited by Glenda Abramson. Routledge.

Cohen, Yolande. 2014c. "Retours sur un depart : de Meknès à Montréal." *Daedalus* 5: 143–158.

Cohen, Yolande. 2015a. "Les mots d'une migration postcoloniale dans les récits de Juifs Montréalais." *Revue d'histoire d'Amérique française*. 69 (1–2): 51–76.

Cohen, Yolande. 2015b. "Souvenirs des départs de juifs du Maroc au Canada." In *Migrations maghrébines comparées : genre, ethnicité et religions*, edited by Yolande Cohen, Mireille Calle Gruber, and Elodie Vignon. Riveneuve.

Cohen, Yolande. 2016. "Une 'installation réussie' à Montréal ? Témoignages de migrants juifs du Maroc." *Diasporas* 27: 101–119.

Cohen, Yolande. 2017. "Retours sur un depart : de Meknès à Montréal." In *Écritures migrantes du genre*, edited by Mireille Calle-Gruber and Sarah Anaïs Crevier Goulet, 233–248. Paris: Presses de l'Université Sorbonne-Nouvelle.

Cohen, Yolande. 2019. "Zionism, Colonialism and Post-Colonial Migrations: Moroccan Jews' Memories of Displacement." *Contemporary Review of the Middle East* 6 (3–4): 1–14.

Cohen, Yolande. 2020a. "Forgetting and Forging: My Canadian Experience as a Moroccan Jew." In *No Better Home? Jews, Canada and the Sense of Belonging*, edited by David S. Koffman, 67–90. Toronto: University of Toronto Press.

Cohen, Yolande. 2020b. "Enclaves ethniques et stratégies résidentielles des juifs à Montréal et Toronto." *Canadian Jewish Studies / Études juives canadiennes* 30: 83–114.

Cohen, Yolande. 2020c. "Établissement de juifs sépharades à Montréal." In *Déracinés, exilés, rapatriés ? Fins d'empires coloniaux et migrations*, edited by Olivier Dard, and Anne Dulphy. Peter Lang.

Cohen, Yolande. 2022. "A Piece of a Torah Scroll in my Basement." *Canadian Jewish Studies / Études juives canadiennes* 33: 173–176.

Cohen, Yolande, and Valérie Assan. 2020. "Circulations et migrations des juifs du Maghreb en France de la fin de la première guerre mondiale aux années 1960. Introduction." *Archives juives* 53 (1): 4–15.

Cohen, Yolande, and Aomar Boum. 2024. "Moroccan Jews' Migration Through France: From Camp to Camp (1948–1956)." UCLA, https://www.youtube.com/watch?v=KsI1NDbLn6w. 2024.

Cohen, Yolande, and Adriana Brodsky. 2024. "Argentina and Canada: A Promised Land for Moroccan Jews?" In *Promised Lands North and South: Jewish Canada and Jewish Argentina in Conversation*, edited by David S. Koffman and David M. K. Sheinin, 55–71. Brill.

Cohen, Yolande, and Christine Chevalier-Caron. 2019. "La langue française chez les sépharades du Québec : une stratégie de préservation culturelle et d'intégration sociale (1960–1980)." *Historical Studies in Education/Revue d'histoire de l'éducation* 31 (1): 93–112.

Cohen, Yolande, and Christine Chevalier Caron. 2020. "Imaginaire colonial et reconfigurations du judaïsme en France : une régénération ?" *Archives juives* 53 (1): 103–126.

Cohen, Yolande, and Christine Chevalier Caron. 2023. "La 'renaissance' du judaïsme français après la Shoah (1945–1970)." *Diasporas* (41). https://doi.org/10.4000/diasporas.14070.

Cohen, Yolande, and Samia Dumais. 2023. "Antisémitisme et discriminations perçues par des Juif.ve.s du Maroc à Montréal." *Canadian Jewish Studies / Études juives canadiennes* 35 (Spring): 40–64.

Cohen, Yolande, and Linda Guerry. 2011. "Mariages et parcours migratoires : juifs nés au Maroc et mariés à la Spanish and Portuguese Synagogue de Montréal (1969–1981)." *Studies in Religion/Études religieuses* 40 (3): 293–317.

Cohen, Yolande, and Noureddine Harrami. 2018. "From Synagogue to Mosque: My Grand-Father's House in the Old Mellah of Meknes." In *Homelands and Diasporas: Perspectives on Jewish Culture in the Mediterranean and Beyond*, edited by Dario Miccoli, Marcella Simoni, and Giorgia Foscarini, 26–40. Newcastle upon Tyne: Cambridge Scholars Publishing.

Cohen, Yolande, and Evens Jabouin. 2021. "Comparer l'incomparable ? Haïtiens et juifs marocains en France (1960–1980)." *Archives juives* 54 (2): 112–132.

Cohen, Yolande, and Nicolas Jodoin. 2021. "Entre l'ancien mellah et le nouveau mellah de Meknès : mobilités urbaines et modernité durant l'entre-deux-guerre." In *Histoire contemporaine du Maroc. Passé et temps présent*, Vol. 1 edited by Khalid Ben-Srhir, 181–206. Publications de la faculté des lettres et sciences humaines de Rabat, Maroc.

Cohen, Yolande, and Joseph Yossi Lévy. 1995. "Élites et organisation communautaire chez les juifs marocains à Montréal : du soleil à la liberté." *Annuaire de l'émigration*, Rabat, Ministère des communautés marocaines vivant à l'étranger, 320–327.

Cohen, Yolande, and Joseph Yossi Lévy. 1998. "Women in the Moroccan-Jewish Community of Montreal." In *From Memory to Transformation: Jewish Women's Voices*, edited by Sarah Silberstein Swartz and Margie Wolfe, translated by Myriam Jarsky, 267–275. Toronto: Second Story Press.

Cohen, Yolande, and Joseph Yossi Lévy. 2000. CD-ROM *Juifs marocains : traditions et modernité*.

Cohen, Yolande, and Martin Messika. 2012. "Sharing and Unsharing Memories of Jews of Moroccan Origin in Montréal and Paris Compared." *Quest. Issues in Contemporary Jewish History* 4 (November): 32–52.

Cohen, Yolande, and Martin Messika. 2023. "Marriage and Mobility of Moroccan Jews in Montreal and Paris." In *The Ever-Dying People?: Canada's Jews in Comparative Perspective*, edited by Robert Brym, Randal F. Schnoor, 318–333. Toronto: University of Toronto Press.

Cohen, Yolande, Martin Messika, and Sara Cohen Fournier. 2015. "Memories of Departures: Stories of Jews from Muslim Lands in Montreal." In *Beyond Testimony and Trauma: Oral History in the Aftermath of Mass Violence*, edited by Steven High, 311–331. Vancouver: UBC Press.

Cohen, Yolande, and Philippe Néméh-Nombré. 2019. "Le Conseil national des femmes juives du Canada et l'accueil des femmes juives d'Afrique du Nord au Québec au xxe siècle : une mé-rencontre." *Revue de l'Institut des langues et cultures d'Europe, Amérique, Afrique, Asie et Australie* (34) : 1–22.

Cohen, Yolande, and Stephanie Tara Schwartz. 2017. "Scholarship on Moroccan Jews in Canada: Multidisciplinary, Multilingual and Diasporic." *Journal of Canadian Studies* 50 (3): 1–21.

Cohen, Yolande, and Yann Scioldo-Zurcher. 2012. "Migrations juives maghrébines à Paris et Montréal : approche quantitative du mariage religieux en migration, 1954–1980." In *La bienvenue et l'adieu : migrants juifs et musulmans au Maghreb. xve-xxe siècles. Vol. 2*, edited by F. Abécassis, K. Dirèche, and R. Aouad, 181–204. Paris/Casablanca, Karthala: La croisée des chemins.

Cohen, Yolande, and Yann Scioldo-Zürcher. 2014. "Maghrebi Jewish Migrations and Religious Marriage in Paris and Montreal, 1954–1980." In *Religion in the Public Sphere*, edited by Solange Lefebvre and Lori Beaman, 250–274. Toronto: University of Toronto Press.

Cohen, Yolande and Émilien Tortel. 2025. "Delegation and Control: France and the Transit of Moroccan Jews (1948-1954)." *North African studies*: 1–25.

General Bibliography

Jews in Morocco and North-Africa

Abécassis, Frédéric, Karima Dirèche, and Rita Aouad, eds. 2012. *La bienvenue et l'adieu : migrants juifs et musulmans au Maghreb. xve-xxe siècles*. Paris/Casablanca, Karthala: La croisée des chemins.

Abécassis, Frédéric, and Jean-François Faü. 2011. "Les juifs dans le monde musulman à l'âge des nations (1840–1945)." In *Les juifs dans l'histoire*, edited by Antoine Germa, Benjamin Lellouch, and Evelyne Patlagean, 545–570. Paris: Champs Vallon.

Abitbol, Michel. 1980. *Judaïsme d'Afrique du Nord xixe–xxe siècles*. Jérusalem: Institut Ben-Zvi pour la recherche sur les communautés Juives d'Orient, Publication du Centre de Recherche sur les Juifs d'Afrique du Nord et Université Hébraïque.
Abitbol, Michel. 1989. *The Jews of North Africa During the Second World War*. Detroit: Wayne State University Press.
Abitbol, Michel. 2009. *Histoire du Maroc*. Paris: Perrin.
Abitbol, Michel. 2010. "Decolonization and Independence: Its Impact in North-Africa." In *History of Alliance Israélite Universelle*, edited by Kaspi. Paris, France: Armand Colin.
Balhoul, Joëlle. 1983. *Le culte de la table dressée, rites et traditions de la table juive algérienne*. Paris: Métailié.
Bar-Asher, Shalom, ed. 1977. *The Taqanot of the Jews in Morocco*. Jerusalem: Zalman Shazar Center.
Bensimon-Donath, Doris. 1968. *Évolution du judaïsme marocain sous le Protectorat français, 1912–1956*. Paris: Mouton.
Bilu, Yoram, and André Levy. 1997. "Nostalgia and Ambivalence: The Reconstruction of Jewish-Muslim Relations in Oulad Mansour." In *Sephardi and Middle Eastern Jewries: History and Culture in the Modern Era*, edited by Harvey Goldberg, 288–311. Bloomington: Indiana University Press.
Bin-Nun, Y. 2004. "Psychosis or an Ability to Foresee the Future? The Contribution of the World Jewish Organizations to the Establishment of Rights for Jews in Independent Morocco, 1955–1961." *REEH* (10): 25–67.
Boum, Aomar. 2013. *Memories of Absence: How Muslims Remember Jews in Morocco*. Stanford, CA: Stanford University Press.
Colloque international sur la communauté juive marocaine. 1980. *Juifs du Maroc, identité et dialogue*. Grenoble: La Pensée sauvage.
Elbaz, Mikhaël. 2001. "Pariahs, Arrivists and Rebels. Jews of Morocco and Moroccan Jews." In *The Unruly: Jews, Moroccans, Rebels*, 23–65. Paris, France: Desclée de Brouwer.
Gerber, Jane. 1980. *Jewish Society in Fez*. Leiden: Brill.
Gilson Miller, Susan. 2011. "Making Tangier Modern: Ethnicity and Urban Development, 1880–1930." In *Jewish Culture and Society in North Africa*, edited by Emily Benichou Gottreich and Daniel J. Schroeter, 128–149. Bloomington: Indiana University Press.
Goldberg, Harvey, ed. 1996. *Sephardi and Middle Eastern Jewries. History and Culture in the Modern Era*. Bloomington: Indiana University Press.
Gottreich, Emily. 2007. *The Mellah of Marrakesh: Jewish and Muslim Space in Morocco's Red City*. Bloomington: Indiana University Press.
Gottreich, Emily, and Daniel J. Schroeter, eds. 2011. *Jewish Culture and Society in North Africa*. Bloomington: Indiana University Press.
Heller-Goldenberg, Lucette, ed. 2004. *Les séfarades du Maghreb*. Köln: La Fourmi.

Hoisington, William A. 1984. *The Casablanca Connection: French Colonial Policy, 1936–1943*. Chapel Hill: University of North Carolina Press.

Kably, Mohamed. 2013. *Histoire du Maroc*. Rabat: Publications de l'Institut royal pour la recherche sur l'histoire du Maroc.

Kenbib, Mohammed. 1994. *Juifs et musulmans au Maroc, 1859–1948*. Rabat: Université Mohammed V, Faculté des lettres et des sciences humaines.

Kenbib, Mohammed. 1996. *Les protégés. Contribution à l'histoire contemporaine du Maroc*. Casablanca: Publication de la Faculté des lettres et des sciences humaines de l'Université Mohammed V.

Kosansky, Oren. 2016. "When Jews Speak Arabic: Dialectology and Difference in Colonial Morocco." *Comparative Studies in Society and History* 58 (1): 5–39.

Laskier, Michael M. 1994. *North African Jewry in the Twentieth Century: The Jews of Morocco, Tunisia and Algeria*. New York: New York University Press.

Lasry, Jean-Claude, and Claude Tapia. 1989. *Les juifs du Maghreb: diasporas contemporaines*. Paris; Montréal: L'Harmattan; Presses de l'Université de Montréal.

Loupo, Yaacov. 2006. *Métamorphose ultra-orthodoxe chez les juifs du Maroc*. Paris: L'Harmattan.

Memmi, Albert. [1957] 1985. *Portrait du colonisé : (précédé de) Portrait du colonisateur*. Paris: Gallimard.

Miller, Susan Gilson. 2013. *A History of Modern Morocco*. Cambridge: Cambridge University Press.

Reeva, S. Simon, Michael M. Laskier, and Sara Reguer, eds. 2003. *The Jews of the Middle East and North Africa in Modern Times*. New York: Columbia University Press.

Rivet, Daniel. 2002. *The Maghrib Confronted to the Colonization*. Paris, France: Hachette.

Rodrigue, Aron. 2003. *Jews and Muslims: Images of Sephardi and Eastern Jewries*. Seattle: University of Washington Press.

Schroeter, Daniel J. 2002. *The Sultan's Jew: Morocco and the Sephardi World*. Stanford, CA: Stanford University Press.

Schroeter, Daniel J. 2008. "The Shifting Boundaries of Moroccan Jewish Identities." *Jewish Social Studies: History, Culture, Society* 15 (1): 145–164.

Senhadji Khiat, Dalila. 2010. "Les mosquées en Algérie ou l'espace reconquis : l'exemple d'Oran." In *L'année du Maghreb*, vol. 6., edited by Daniel Schroeter and Emily Gottreich. *Jewish Culture and Society in North Africa*. Bloomington: Indiana University Press.

Stillman, Norman A. 1979. *The Jews of Arab Lands*. Philadelphia: The Jewish Publication of America.

Stillman, Norman A. 1996. "Middle Eastern and North African Jewries Confront Modernity: Orientation, Disorientation, Reorientation." In *Sephardi and*

Middle Eastern Jewries: History and Culture in the Modern Era, edited by Harvey Goldberg, 59–72. Bloomington: Indiana University Press.
Taïeb, Jacques. 1979. "Historique d'un exode : l'émigration des juifs du Maghreb de la fin des années quarante à nos jours." *Yod* (10): 88–100.
Tolédano-Attias, Ruth. 2009. "La dénaturalisation des juifs d'Egypte." In *The End of Judaism in Muslim Countries*, edited by Shmuel Trigano. Paris, France: Denoël.
Trevisan Semi, Emanuela. 2010. "Double Trauma and Manifold Narratives: Jews' and Muslims' Representations of the Departure of Moroccan Jews in the 1950s and 1960s." *Journal of Modern Jewish Studies* 9 (1): 107–125.
Trevisan Semi, Emanuela, and Hanane Sekkat Hatimi. 2015. *Mémoire et représentations des juifs au Maroc : les voisins absents de Meknès*. Paris: Publisud.
Trigano, Hélène, and Shmuel Trigano, eds. 2000. *La mémoire sépharade. Entre l'oubli et l'avenir*. Paris: In Press.
Trigano, Shmuel. 2009. *La fin du judaïsme en terres d'Islam*. Paris, France: Denoël.
Tsur, Yaron. 1995. *The Jews of Casablanca: A Study of Modernization in a Colonial Jewish Society*. Tel Aviv: The Open University Press.
Tsur, Yaron. 2001. *A Torn Community: The Jews of Morocco and Nationalism 1943–1954*. Tel Aviv: Am Oved. [Hebrew]
Tsur, Yaron. 2007. "The Brief Career of Prosper Cohen: A Sectorial Analysis of the North African Jewish Leadership in the Early Years of Israeli Statehood." *Studies in Contemporary Jewry* 22: 67–72.
Valensi, Lucette. 2002. "Multicultural Visions: The Cultural Tapestry of the Jews of North Africa." In *Cultures of the Jews: A New History*, edited by David Biale, 887–932. New York: Schocken Books.
Valensi, Lucette. 2005. "L'horizon culturel des juifs d'Afrique du Nord." In *La culture des juifs : une nouvelle histoire*, edited by David Biale, 781–820. Paris; Tel-Aviv: Édition de l'Éclat.
Vermeren, Pierre. 2012. *Misère de l'historiographie du Maghreb post-colonial : 1962–2012*. Paris: Publications de la Sorbonne.

French Jewishness and Maghrebi Migrations

Bensimon-Donath, Doris. 1971. *L'intégration des juifs nord-africains en France*. Paris: Mouton.
Kaspi, André, and Valérie Assan, eds. 2010. *Histoire de l'Alliance israélite universelle, de 1860 à nos jours*. Paris: Armand Colin.
Mandel, Maud. 2014. *Muslims and Jews in France: History of a Conflict*. Princeton, NJ: Princeton University Press.
Poirier, Véronique. 1998. *Ashkénazes et séfarades : une étude comparée de leurs relations en France et en Israël : années 1950–1990*. Paris: Les Éditions du Cerf.

Taïeb, Jacques. 2010. "Immigrés d'Afrique du Nord: Combien? Quand? Pourquoi?." In *Terre d'exil, terre d'asile. Migrations juives en France aux XIXe et XXe siècles*, edited by Colette Zytniki, 149–154. Paris: Éditions de l'Éclat.

Tsur, Yaron. 2001. "The Alliance Israelite Universelle and Moroccan Judaism in 1949: The Rising of a New Political Path." *Archives juives* 1 (34): 54–73.

Zytnicki, Colette. 1998. *Les juifs à Toulouse entre 1945 et 1970 : une communauté toujours recommencée*. Toulouse: Presses universitaires du Mirail.

Zytnicki, Colette. 2003. "Gérer la rupture : les institutions sociales juives de France face aux migrations des juifs tunisiens (1950–1970)." In *Juifs et musulmans en Tunisie*, edited by Sonia Fellous, 333–342. Paris: Somogy.

Zytnicki, Colette. 2005. "Du rapatrié au séfarade. L'intégration des juifs d'Afrique du Nord dans la société française : essai de bilan." *Archives juives* 38 (2): 84–102.

Canadian and Quebec Jews

Abella, Irving, and Harold Troper. 1982. *None Is Too Many: Canada and the Jews of Europe, 1933–1948*. Toronto: Lester & Orpen Dennys.

Adelman, Howard, and Pierre Anctil. 2011. *Religion, Culture, and the State: Reflections on the Bouchard-Taylor Report*. Toronto: University of Toronto Press.

Adelman, Howard, and John H. Simpson, eds. 1996. *Multiculturalism, Jews and Identities in Canada*. Jerusalem: Magnes Press, The Hebrew University.

Amber, Phyllis, and Irene Lipper. 1968. "Towards an Understanding of Moroccan Jewish Family Life." Master's thesis, McGill University.

Anctil, Pierre, and Gary Caldwell. 1984. *Juifs et réalités juives au Québec*. Quebec: Institut québécois de recherche sur la culture.

Anctil, Pierre, Ira Robinson, and Gérard Bouchard, eds. 2000. *Juifs et Canadiens français dans la société québécoise*. Sillery: Septentrion.

Batshaw, Huguette, and Beverly Lowe. 1971. "The Integration of Moroccan Jewish Immigrants in Montreal (1964–1970)." Master's thesis, McGill University.

Bédard, Jean-Luc. 2005. "Se souvenir, dire, devenir. Constructions de la mémoire chez des générations de sépharades à Montréal." PhD thesis, Université Laval.

Bédard, Jean-Luc. 2007. "Mouvances identitaires et restructuration de soi et des autres parmi des judéo-marocains à Montréal." In *Identités sépharades et modernité*, edited by Jean-Claude Lasry, Joseph Lévy, and Yolande Cohen, 175–190. Quebec: Presses de l'Université de Laval.

Benaïm Ouaknine, Esther. 1976. "L'intégration des juifs marocains au Canada, Monographie de la communauté juive à Montréal." PhD thesis, Université de la Sorbonne Paris.

Benaïm Ouaknine, Esther. 1977. "Une diaspora juive : les Marocains au Québec, dispersion et unite." *Jérusalem* (17): 134–145.
Benaïm Ouaknine, Esther. 1979. "Paradoxe d'un juif, mémoire et devenir des sépharades au Québec." *Les temps modernes* (394): 410–422.
Bensoussan, David, ed. 2010. *Anthologie des écrivains sépharades du Québec*. Montréal: Éditions du Marais.
Bensoussan, David, ed. 2010. *50 ans ensemble : Le livre sépharade 1959–2009*. Montréal: Communauté sépharade unifiée du Québec.
Berdugo-Cohen, Marie, Yolande Cohen, and Joseph Lévy. 1987. *Juifs marocains à Montréal : témoignages d'une immigration modern*. Montreal: Vlb éditeur.
Berman, Gerald, Daphne Nahmiash, and Carol Osmer. 1970. "A Profile of Moroccan Jewish Immigration in Montreal 1957–1967." Master's thesis, McGill University, School of Social Work.
Bialystok, Franklin. 2000. *Delayed Impact: The Holocaust and the Canadian Jewish Community*. Kingston and Montreal: McGill-Queen's University Press.
Blaustein, Esther I., Rachel A. Esar, and Evelyn Miller. 1971. "Spanish and Portuguese Synagogue (Shearith Israel) Montreal, 1768–1968." *The Jewish Historical Society of England Transactions* (23): 11–42.
Boussouga, Hakima. 2003. "La vitalité ethnolinguistique de la communauté juive marocaine de Montréal." Master's thesis, Université du Québec à Montréal.
Brière, Céline. 1990. "Les juifs sépharades à Montréal : traces passagères et marqueurs spatiaux d'une minorité dans une métropole nord-américaine." Master's thesis, Université d'Angers.
Brotman, Ruth C. 1975. *Pauline Donalda: The Life and Career of a Canadian Prima Donna*. Montreal: Eagle Publishing.
Brown, Michael. 1987. *Jew or Juif ? Jews, French-Canadians, and Anglo-Canadians, 1759–1914*. Philadelphia, PA: The Jewish Publication Society.
Brown, Michael. 2007. "Canadian Jews and Multiculturalism: Myths and Realities." *Jewish Political Studies Review* 19 (3–4): 57–75.
Brown, Michael, Richard Menkis, Benjamin Schlesinger, and Stuart Schoenfeld, eds. 1999–2000. *Jews and Judaism in Canada: A Bibliography of Works Published Since 1965*. Toronto: Association for Canadian Jewish Studies / Études juives canadiennes (7–8).
Brym, Robert J., William Shaffir, and Morton Weinfeld, eds. 1993. *The Jews in Canada*. Toronto: Oxford University Press.
Brym, Robert, Keith Neuman, and Rhonda Lenton. 2019. *2018 Survey of Jews in Canada: Final Report*. Toronto: Environics Institute for Survey Research.
Burgard, Antoine. 2017. "Les sépharades dans les études démographiques." In *Les sépharades du Québec : parcours d'exils nord-africains*, edited by Yolande Cohen, 35–56. Montreal: Del Busso.

Byers, Michele, and Stephanie Tara Schwartz. 2013. "Theorizing Multicultural Jewish Identity in Canada." In *Critical Inquiries: A Reader in Studies of Canada*, edited by Lynn Caldwell, Darryl Leroux, and Carrianne Leung, 71–83. Black Point, NS: Fernwood.

Cohen, Judith. 1982. "Judeo-Spanish Traditional Songs in Montreal and Toronto." *Canadian Folk Music Journal* (10): 40–47.

Cohen, Judith. 1989a. "Judeo-Spanish Song in the Sephardic Communities of Montreal and Toronto." PhD thesis, Université de Montréal.

Cohen, Judith. 1989b. "'Ya salió de la mar': Judeo-Spanish Wedding Songs Among Moroccan Jews in Canada." In *Women and Music in Cross-Cultural Perspective*, edited by Ellen Koskoff, 55–68. Urbana: University of Illinois Press.

Dahab, Elizabeth. 2009. *Voices of Exile in Contemporary Canadian Francophone Literature*. Lanham, MD: Lexington Books.

Davies, Alan, ed. 1992. *Antisemitism in Canada: History and Interpretation*. Waterloo, ON: Wilfrid Laurier University Press.

Dinelle, Johanne, and Andrée Barnette-Dalphond. 1985. "Femmes et judaïsme : les femmes immigrantes sépharades à Montréal." Master's thesis, Université du Québec à Montréal.

Draper, Paula J., and Janice B. Karlinsky. 1986. "Abraham's Daughters: Women, Charity and Power in the Canadian Jewish Community." In *Looking into My Sister's Eyes: An Exploration in Women's History*, edited by Jean Burnet, 75–90. Toronto: Multicultural History Society of Ontario.

Eidelman, Jay. 2003. "Kissing Cousins: The Early History of Congregations Shearith Israel of New York City and Montreal." In *Not Written in Stone: Jews, Constitutions and Constitutionalism in Canada*, edited by Daniel Elazar, Michael Brown, and Ira Robinson, 71–83. Ottawa: University of Ottawa Press.

Elbaz, André. 1988. *Sépharadisme d'hier et de demain : trois autobiographies d'immigrants Juifs marocains*. Ottawa: Musée Canadien des civilisations.

Elbaz, Mikhaël. 1986. "Entre l'errance et l'espoir : les juifs à Montréal." *Forces* (73): 58–61.

Elbaz, Mikhaël. 1989. "D'immigrants à ethniques : analyse comparée des pratiques sociales et identitaires des sépharades et ashkénazes à Montréal." In *Les juifs du Maghreb*, Diasporas Journal of Canadian Studies / Revue d'études canadiennes contemporaines, edited by Jean-Claude Lasry and Claude Tapia, 79–101. Montreal: Presses de l'Université de Montréal.

Elbaz, Mikhaël. 1993. "Les héritiers. Générations et identités chez les Juifs sépharades à Montréal." *Revue européene des migrations internationales* 9 (3): 13–34.

Filion, Fernand G. 1979. "La communauté sépharade de Montréal. Une analyse ethno-historique des structures communautaires." PhD thesis, Université Laval.

Gagnon, Alain G. ed. 2010. *La diversité québécoise en débat : Bouchard, Taylor et les autres*. Montreal: Québec Amérique.

Gilzmer, Mechtild. 2010. "La littérature sépharade au Québec." In *Orient lointain—proche Orient, la présence d'Israël dans la littérature francophone*, edited by Till R. Kuhnle, Carmen Oszi, and Saskia Widner, 135–142. Tübingen, Germany: Editions Lendemains 15, Narr Verlag.

Greenstein, Michael. 1989. *Third Solitudes: Tradition and Discontinuity in Jewish-Canadian Literature*. Kingston and Montreal: McGill-Queen's University Press.

Koffman, David S. 2013. "Canadian Jewish Studies since 1999: The State of the Field." In *Canada's Jews: In Time, Space and Spirit*, edited by Ira Robinson, 402–426. Boston: Academic Studies Press.

Lang, Jonathan. 2012. "Shalom Québec: Reappraising the Role of Language in the Integration of Jewish Communities in Montreal." Master's thesis, Université de Montréal.

Langlais, Jacques, and David Rome. 1986. *Juifs et Québécois français : 200 ans d'histoire commune*. Montreal: Fides.

Lash, Shari Rochelle. 1980. "Mobilité professionnelle chez les immigrants juifs nord-africains à Montréal." *Applied Psychology* 29 (1–2): 17–30.

Lash, Shari Rochelle. 2007. "Fitting under the Marriage Canopy: Same-Sex Weddings as Rites of Conformity in a Canadian Liberal Jewish Context." Master's thesis, Wilfrid Laurier University.

Lasry, Jean-Claude. 1980. "Mobilité professionnelle chez les immigrants juifs nord-africains à Montréal." *Applied Psychology* 29 (1–2): 17–33.

Lasry, Jean-Claude. 1981. "A Francophone Diaspora in Quebec." In *The Canadian Jewish Mosaic*, edited by Morton Weinfeld, William Shaffir, and Irwin Cotler, 221–240. Toronto: J. Wiley & Sons Canada.

Lasry, Jean-Claude. 1983. "Sephardim and Ashkenazim in Montréal." In *The Jews in Canada*, edited by Robert Brym, William Shaffir, and Morton Weinfeld, 26–33. Toronto: Oxford University Press.

Lasry, Jean-Claude. 1989. "Essor et tradition : la communauté juive nord-africaine au Québec." In *Les juifs du Maghreb : diasporas contemporaines*, edited by Jean-Claude Lasry and Claude Tapia, 17–54. Paris: L'Harmattan.

Lasry, Jean-Claude, Joseph Lévy, and Yolande Cohen, eds. 2007. *Identités sépharades et modernité*. Quebec: Presses Université de Laval.

La voix sépharade. *Communauté sépharade unifiée du Québec*, ed. 2009. "50 ans d'histoire." Special issue, La voix sépharade (July-August). Montréal.

Légaré, Maurice. 1965. "La population juive de Montréal est-elle victime d'une ségrégation qu'elle se serait elle-même imposée?" *Recherches sociographiques* 4 (3): 312–325.

Lévy, Joseph, and Micheline Labelle. 1995. *Ethnicité et enjeux sociaux : le Québec vu par les leaders de groupes ethnoculturels*. Montreal: Liber.

Manac'h, Julie. 2006. "(Re-)construction de l'identité sépharade de 1998 à nos jours : étude de deux revues communautaires, Los Muestros et La voix sépharade." Master's thesis, Université Rennes 2, Haute-Bretagne.

Menkis, Richard. 2011. "Jewish Communal Identity at the Crossroads: Early Jewish Responses to Canadian Multiculturalism, 1963–1965." *Studies in Religion / Sciences Religieuses* 40 (3): 283–292.

Menkis, Richard, and Norman Ravvin. 2004. *The Canadian Jewish Studies Reader*. Calgary: Red Deer Press.

Messika, Martin. 2020. *Politiques de l'accueil : états et associations face à la migration juive du Maghreb en France et au Canada des années 1950 à la fin des années 1970*. Rennes: Presses universitaires de Rennes.

Messika, Martin, and Yolande Cohen. 2017. "Juifs marocains à Paris et à Montréal." In *Les sépharades du Québec : parcours d'exils nord-africains*, edited by Yolande Cohen, 57–71. Montreal: Del Busso.

Miles, William F. S. 2012. "Between Ashkenaz and Québécois: Fifty Years of Francophone Sephardim in Montréal." *Diaspora* 16 (1–2): 29–66.

Mills, Sean. 2010. *The Empire Within: Postcolonial Thought and Political Activism in Sixties Montreal*. Kingston and Montreal: McGill-Queen's University Press.

Moldofsky, Naomi. 1968. "The Economic Adjustment of North African Jewish Immigrants in Montreal." PhD thesis, McGill University.

Néméh-Nombré, Philippe. 2017. "L'emploi des femmes judéo-marocaines à leur arrivée à Montréal (1956–1978)." In *Les sépharades du Québec : parcours d'exils nord-africains*, edited by Yolande Cohen, 161–182. Montreal: Del Busso.

Olazabal, Ignaki. 2000. "Entre les processus de communalisation et d'intersystème; juifs et Québécois francophones à Montréal à travers quatre générations." In *Juifs et Canadiens français dans la société québécoise*, edited by Pierre Anctil, Ira Robinson, and Gérard Bouchard, 107–126. Sillery: Septentrion.

Pâquet, Martin. 1997. *Vers un ministère québécois de l'immigration, 1945–1968*. Ottawa: Société Historique du Canada.

Pâquet, Martin. 2005. *Tracer les marges de la cite : étranger, immigrant et État au Québec, 1627–1981*. Montreal: Boréal.

Redouane, Najib. 2004. "L'aventure collective des voix littéraires sépharades au Canada." *International Journal of Francophone Studies* 7 (1): 51–65.

Roda, Jessica. 2015. "Pop Stars as Ambassador of the Sephardic Culture at the Festival Sefarad in Montreal." *Contemporary Jewry* 35 (1): 73–88.

Rome, David. 1974. *Early Documents on the Canadian Jewish Congress 1914–1921*. Montreal: Canadian Jewish Congress.

Rome, David. 1975. *Inventory of Documents on the Jewish School Question 1903–1921*. Montreal: Canadian Jewish Congress.

Sadock, Johann. 2006. "Assignations et stratégies d'identification à l'Orient chez les écrivains juifs francophones du Québec." In *Identités hybrides*.

Orient et orientalisme au Québec, edited by Mounia Benlalil and Janusz Przychoden, 141–159. Montreal: Presses de l'Université de Montréal.

Sawa, Suzanne Myers. 1991. "The Odyssey of Dahlia Obadia: Morocco, Israel, Canada." *Canadian Folk Music Journal* (19): 32–39.

Schnoor, Randal F. 2011. "The Contours of Canadian Jewish Life." *Contemporary Jewry* 31 (3): 179–197.

Shaffir, William. 2001. "Fieldwork among Hasidic Jews: Moral Challenges and Missed Opportunities." *Jewish Journal of Sociology* 43 (1–2): 53–69.

Shaffir, William. 2002. "Outremont's Hasidim and Their Neighbors: An Eruv and Its Repercussions." *Jewish Journal of Sociology* 44 (1–2): 56–71.

Shaffir, William. 2004. "Secular Studies in a Hasidic Enclave: 'What Do We Need It For?'" *The Jewish Journal of Sociology* 46 (1–2): 59–77.

Shahar, Charles. 2015. *2011 National Household Survey: The Jewish Community of Montreal. Part 7, The Sephardic Community.* Montreal: Jewish Federations of Canada—CJA.

Shahar, Charles, and Elisabeth Perez. 2002. *Analyse du recensement de 2001.* Montreal: Fédération CJA.

Sourisce, Nicolas. 1996. "La Communauté juive montréalaise : enracinement original." Master's thesis, Université d'Angers.

Taïeb-Carlen, Sarah. 1996. "Les femmes sépharades et leur integration à Toronto." *Canadian Woman Studies / Les cahiers de la femme* 16 (4): 91–94.

Tapia, Claude. 2007. "Les migrations sépharades après la seconde guerre mondiale : mutations culturelles, idéologiques et modes d'adaptations." In *Identités sépharades et modernité,* edited by Jean-Claude Lasry, Joseph Lévy, and Yolande Cohen, 175–190. Quebec: Presses Université de Laval.

Train, Kelly Amanda. 2008. "Authenticity, Identity and the Politics of Belonging: Sephardic Jews from North Africa and India Within the Toronto Jewish Community." PhD thesis, York University.

Train, Kelly Amanda. 2013. "Am I That Jew? North African Jewish Experience in the Toronto Jewish Day School System and the Establishment of Or Haemet Sephardic School." *Diaspora, Indigenous, and Minority Education* 7 (1): 6–20.

Tulchinsky, Gerald. 1992. *Taking Root: The Origins of the Canadian Jewish Community.* Toronto: Lester Publishing Limited.

Tulchinsky, Gerald. 1998. *Branching Out: The Transformations of the Canadian Jewish Community.* Toronto: Stoddart.

Tulchinsky, Gerald. 2008. *Canada's Jews: A People's Journey.* Toronto: University of Toronto Press.

Vigod, Bernard L. 1984. *Les juifs au Canada.* Ottawa: Société historique du Canada.

Weinfeld, Morton, William Shaffir, and Irwin Cotler, eds. 1981. *The Canadian Jewish Mosaic.* Toronto: J. Wiley & Sons Canada.

Wolfman, Oscar. 2002. "Remaking Family: Canadian Jews, Sexuality, and Relationships." In *Queer Jews*, edited by David Shneer and Caryn Aviv, 156–171. New York: Routledge.

Migratory Circulations and Sephardi Diasporas

Akhtar, Salman. 1999. "The Immigrant, the Exile, and the Nostalgia." *Journal of Applied Psychoanalytic Studies* 1 (2): 123–130.

Bensimon-Donath, Doris. 1970. *Immigrants d'Afrique du Nord en Israël*. Paris: Éditions Anthropos.

Biale, David. 2002. *Cultures of the Jews: A New History*. New York: Schocken Books.

Bordes-Benayoun, Chantal. 2002. "Les territoires de la diaspora judéo-marocaine postcoloniale." *Diasporas. Histoire et sociétés* (2): 1–14.

Bordes-Benayoun, Chantal, and Dominique Schnapper. 2006. *Diasporas et nations*. Paris: Editions Odile Jacob.

Bouchard, Gérard. 2011. "Qu'est ce que l'interculturalisme?" *McGill Law Journal* 56 (2): 395–468.

Chetrit, Shmuel S. 2004. *The Mizrahi Struggle in Israel: 1948–2003*. Tel Aviv, Israel: Am-Oved. [Hebrew]

Elkaïm, Betty. 1981. "Evaluations des séquelles psychologiques du deuil." Master's thesis, Université de Montréal.

Goldberg, Harvey. 2008. "From Sephardi to Mizrahi and Back Again: Changing Meanings of 'Sephardi' in Its Social Environment." *Jewish Social Studies* 15 (1): 165–188.

Green, Nancy. 2002. *Repenser les migrations*. Paris: Presses universitaires de France.

Haque, Eve. 2012. *Multiculturalism Within a Bilingual Framework: Language, Race, and Belonging in Canada*. Toronto: University of Toronto Press.

Hayes, Saul. 1977. "Are the Jews of Quebec an Endangered Species?" *Canadian Jewish Studies / Études juives canadiennes* 1 (1): 24–34.

Heller-Goldenberg, Lucette. 1997. "Les juifs marocains au Québec: l'exil et le royaume." In *Québec-Canada. Cultures et littératures immigrés*, edited by Peter Klaus, 171–183. Berlin: Institut für Romanische Philologie der Freien Universität Berlin.

Heller-Goldenberg, Lucette. 2004. "Judeo-Moroccan Memory in Quebec." In *Textualizing the Immigrant Experience in Contemporary Quebec*, edited by Susan Ireland and Patrice J. Proulx, 149–159. Westport, CT: Praeger.

High, Steven, et al. 2015. *Beyond Testimony and Trauma: Oral History in the Aftermath of Mass Violence*. Vancouver: UBC Press.

Lasry, Jean-Claude. 1977. "Cross-Cultural Perspectives on Mental Health and Immigration Adaptation." *Social Psychiatry / Sozialpsychiatrie / Psychiatrie sociale* 12 (2): 49–55.

Layman, Lenore. 2009. "Reticence in Oral History Interviews." *Oral History Review* 36 (2): 207–230.

Mays, Devi. 2012. "Playing with Peculiarity: Sephardic Migrations and the Ambiguity of National Identity." PhD thesis, Indiana University.

Rosen, Lawrence. 1984. *Bargaining for Reality: The Construction of Social Relations in a Muslim Community*. Chicago: The University of Chicago Press.

Sarna, M. Nahum. 1989. *The JPS Torah Commentary Exodus*. Philadelphia: Jewish Publication Society.

Schnoor, Randal F. 2006. "Being Gay and Jewish: Negotiating Intersecting Identities." *Sociology of Religion* 67 (1): 43–60.

Sheftel, Anna, and Stacey Zembrzycki. 2010. "Only Human: A Reflection on the Ethical and Methodological Challenges of Working with 'Difficult' Stories." *Oral History Review* 37 (2): 191–214.

Shenhav, Yehouda. 2007. "Modernity and the Hybridization of Nationalism and Religion: Zionism and the Jews of the Middle East as a Heuristic Case." *Theory and Society* 36 (1): 1–30.

Shenhav, Yehouda, and Hannan Hever. 2012. "Arab Jews after Structuralism: Zionist Discourse and the (De)formation of an Ethnic Identity." *Social Identities* 18 (1): 99–116.

Shohat, Ella. 1999. "The Invention of Mizrahim." *Journal of Palestine Studies* 29 (1): 5–20.

Shohat, Ella. 2002. "The Shaping of Mizrahi Studies: A Relational Approach." *Israel Studies Forum* 17 (2): 86–93.

Smooha, Sammy. 1978. *Israel: Pluralism and Conflict*. London: Henley, Routledge and K. Paul.

Tint, Barbara. 2010. "History, Memory, and Intractable Conflict." *Conflict Resolution Quarterly* 27 (3): 239–256.

Tsur, Yaron. 1997. "Carnival Fears: Moroccan Immigrants and the Ethnic Problem in the Young State of Israel." *Journal of Israeli History: Politics, Society, Culture* 18 (1): 73–103.

Weinstock, Nathan. 2007. *Une si longue présence : comment le monde arabe a perdu ses juifs, 1947–1967*. Paris: Plon.

Canadian Studies

Series Editor: Pierre Anctil

The Canadian Studies collection touches upon all aspects of Canadian society in all disciplines with a special focus on Canadian women, cultural and religious minorities, and First Nations. The collection is also devoted to regional studies, local communities, and the unique characteristics of Canadian society. Among the topics privileged in this collection are all contemporary issues, especially in the domain of the environment, with regards to large urban centres and new forms of art and communications.

Previous titles in the *Canadian Studies* Series

David Leadbeater, ed., *Northern Ontario in Historical Statistics, 1871–2021: Expansion, Growth, and Decline in a Hinterland-Colonial Region*, 2024.

Simon-Pierre Lacasse, *Les Juifs de la Révolution tranquille : regards d'une minorité religieuse sur le Québec de 1945 à 1976*, 2022.

Winfried Siemerling, *Les écritures noires du Canada : l'Atlantique noir et la présence du passé*, traduit de l'anglais par Patricia Godbout, 2022.

Pierre Anctil, *History of the Jews in Quebec*, 2021.

Geneviève Bonin-Labelle, ed., *Women in Radio: Unfiltered Voices from Canada*, 2020.

Francis Mus, *The Demons of Leonard Cohen*, 2020.

Pierre Anctil, *A Reluctant Welcome for Jewish People: Voices in* Le Devoir's *Editorials, 1910–1947*, 2019.

Le Mawiomi Mi'gmawei de Gesp'gewa'gi, *Nta'tugwaqanminen – Notre histoire : l'évolution des Mi'gmaqs de Gespe'gewa'gi*, 2018.

Pierre Anctil, *Jacob Isaac Segal: A Montreal Yiddish Poet and His Milieu*, 2017.

Hughes Théorêt, *The Blue Shirts: Adrien Arcand and Fascist Anti-Semitism in Canada*, 2017.

For a complete list of the University of Ottawa Press titles, please visit:
www.Press.uOttawa.ca

www.ingramcontent.com/pod-product-compliance
Lightning Source LLC
Chambersburg PA
CBHW071822230426
43670CB00013B/2535